CW01333500

Decisions That Matter

Also by Adrienne Adhami

Power Hour: How to Focus on Your Goals and Create a Life You Love

Decisions That Matter

How to make decisions in a world of endless choice

Adrienne Adhami

Cornerstone Press

CORNERSTONE PRESS

UK | USA | Canada | Ireland | Australia
India | New Zealand | South Africa

Cornerstone Press is part of the Penguin Random House group of companies whose addresses can be found at global.penguinrandomhouse.com

Penguin Random House UK,
One Embassy Gardens, 8 Viaduct Gardens, London SW11 7BW

penguin.co.uk

Penguin Random House UK

First published 2025
001

Copyright © Adrienne Adhami, 2025

The moral right of the author has been asserted

Penguin Random House values and supports copyright. Copyright fuels creativity, encourages diverse voices, promotes freedom of expression and supports a vibrant culture. Thank you for purchasing an authorised edition of this book and for respecting intellectual property laws by not reproducing, scanning or distributing any part of it by any means without permission. You are supporting authors and enabling Penguin Random House to continue to publish books for everyone. No part of this book may be used or reproduced in any manner for the purpose of training artificial intelligence technologies or systems. In accordance with Article 4(3) of the DSM Directive 2019/790, Penguin Random House expressly reserves this work from the text and data mining exception.

Illustrations on p. 20 and p. 227 by Sammi Adhami
Typeset in 11.2/17pt Calluna by Jouve (UK), Milton Keynes
Printed and bound in Great Britain by Clays Ltd, Elcograf S.p.A.

The authorised representative in the EEA is Penguin Random House Ireland, Morrison Chambers, 32 Nassau Street, Dublin D02 YH68

A CIP catalogue record for this book is available from the British Library

ISBN: 978-1-529-92549-4 (hardback)
ISBN: 978-1-529-92550-0 (trade paperback)

MIX
Paper | Supporting
responsible forestry
FSC® C018179

Penguin Random House is committed to a sustainable future for our business, our readers and our planet. This book is made from Forest Stewardship Council® certified paper.

For Ayeisha and Alex, my beloved comrades.

Contents

Introduction: *Decision-making in the twenty-first century* 1

1 **Rules of Engagement**: *Six fundamental rules for decision-making* 18

2 **Values**: *Value-led decision-making, balancing competing values, creating a rule book* 52

3 **Joy**: *The science of joy, confronting negativity bias* 90

4 **Success**: *Redefining success, seasons of success, the personal ambition paradox* 126

5 **Impact**: *Circles of impact, self-respect & self-sabotage, measuring the impact of decisions* 162

6 **Making Decisions in the Real World**: *Training your decision-making muscle, how to use a decision-making matrix* 204

Conclusion: *Embracing uncertainty, mistakes and regrets* 235

Acknowledgements 253
Notes 255

Introduction

Decision-making in the twenty-first century

For a moment, let's step into a time machine and travel back to 1975. As you step out and take a look around, what can you see? At first you might think people look pretty much the same, but look closer and you'll see that their behaviour is noticeably different. Nobody is taking a selfie, texting on a smartphone, or waiting for an Uber. Need to make a call? You'll have to walk down the street to use the phone booth on the corner. Want to send a message overseas? Well, it could take a week or so for your letter to reach its destination, then you'll have to wait another week or so for a response.

Next, walk into an office and you'll notice that there are no laptops, tablets or smart speakers. Instead, you'll see typewriters, fax machines, paper and pens. Take a look through the window of a house and you'll see a family gathered together around a bulky television set for the nightly news. Getting hungry? You'd better make it to the local shop before it closes at 5 p.m.

What else is going on? Well, afros are in fashion, Queen's

iconic anthem 'Bohemian Rhapsody' is number one in the charts and Harold Wilson is the prime minister. Back in 1975, nobody could have predicted how rapidly the world was about to change or how vastly different our lives would be today.

The 1980s brought us personal computers and video game consoles, transforming the way we work, play and communicate. The 1990s delivered public access to the World Wide Web, the internet exploded and we started sending emails. In July 1995, Jeff Bezos officially launched a website to sell books, called Amazon. This new enterprise marked the beginning of a profound shift in the way we consume products and services, paving the way for e-commerce, same-day delivery and fast fashion.

The technological advances of the twentieth century catapulted us into a world of global connectivity and digitalisation – also known as the Information Era. Suddenly, news, data and information could easily be stored and shared by everyone across the planet. By 2007, we had iPhones in our pockets and we were updating our Facebook statuses daily. And this didn't just alter how we communicate, it influenced almost every aspect of modern life, from how we consume media and entertainment to the way we work.

While the standard work week for full-time employees back in the 1970s was forty hours, the notion of 'work-life balance' wasn't discussed; it was simply how life was lived. For most people, weekends were spent with family and friends, without the intrusion of work demands. With no home

INTRODUCTION

internet connection, employees weren't tethered to their jobs around the clock. When they left the office at the end of the day, they were likely to be disconnected until they returned the next morning. The pace of life and the pace of change was slower.

Today, many industries operate on a 24/7 basis across all time zones, which means the traditional work week no longer exists. In the modern world, working from anywhere means working from everywhere. And it's not just our work schedules that have changed; cultural attitudes have evolved too. The growing emphasis on productivity and efficiency means we now value speed and growth above everything else, often compromising quality for convenience. This increase in pace is evident not only in our work lives but also in our consumption habits and social interactions.

This trend towards immediacy has shaped our behaviours and expectations in profound ways. Instant messages have replaced lengthy face-to-face conversations. We expect instant responses and get frustrated when we have to wait even a few minutes, let alone hours, for a reply. We skim through articles, rush through meals – we even walk faster. When researchers from the British Council and the University of Hertfordshire measured the walking speed of pedestrians in thirty-four cities around the world, they found that the average walking pace was 10 per cent faster than just a decade ago.

Looking back, throughout history there has always been change; what's different now is its breathtaking pace. While the progress and innovation of the past few decades has undeniably enriched our lives in countless ways, it also presents us with a new set of dilemmas. Living in the era of excess is simultaneously reducing our attention and heightening our expectations. We need a new set of skills and strategies for navigating daily life. Quite literally, times have changed, resulting in an existential crisis characterised by overwhelm and indecision.

We are living in the age of abundance, with more choice, opportunity and freedom than ever before. Yet there is a paradox here – it is both a blessing and a curse. Despite the apparent advantages of having multiple options, it often leads to confusion, second-guessing and a persistent sense of dissatisfaction. The sheer volume of information and resources available to us surpasses anything our parents and grandparents could have imagined.

It's estimated that the average person now makes around 35,000 decisions each day. We are spoiled for choice. We can swipe and scroll endlessly through a world of limitless possibilities, from the clothes we buy to the people we date and the careers we pursue. Welcome to decision-making in the twenty-first century. We can do anything, go anywhere and be anyone. So, how do we choose?

The reality is that the more choices we have, the more overwhelmed we become. The more clothes we have hanging in the wardrobe, the harder it is to get dressed. The more things we write on a to-do list, the less likely we are to complete them. The more TV channels we have access to, the longer it takes to make a choice. Did you know that viewers spend an average of 10.5 minutes per day trying to decide what to watch? Assuming that they watch TV every day, that's more than sixty-three hours per year – almost three whole days given to this fairly unimportant decision.

Perhaps another reason many of us feel unsatisfied no matter what we choose is because of the socially reinforced message that we can 'have it all'. We deserve the best. We're worth it. So why settle for anything less? Whether we're planning a holiday, considering a new job or simply ordering dinner in a restaurant, we're told to aim for the best and so our expectations keep going up. We're navigating a minefield of options in pursuit of perfection, all searching for a unicorn. We're so afraid of making the wrong choice, or that there might be a better choice out there, that we end up making no choice at all. We procrastinate and put off committing in case a better option comes along. Then the cycle continues and we find ourselves caught in a trap.

From everyday mundane choices to big life-changing moments, overthinking our decisions is a modern-day challenge that seemingly plagues us all. We overthink yesterday's meeting with our co-workers: *I hope I didn't come across as too demanding.* We overthink which colour to paint the bathroom: *Does Enchanted Eden Green reflect who I really am? Maybe I'm more aligned with Nordic Sky Blue?* We overthink the reply to a text message: *What does 'Okay, sure' really mean? Are they annoyed? Are they being sarcastic? Maybe I should call?*

We repeatedly weigh up the pros and cons, and endlessly analyse the same thing over and over. This issue stems from a variety of sources, including a fear of regret, decision fatigue (the mental exhaustion we feel from making a lot of decisions) and a lack of clarity about our priorities (*What if this? What about that?*). Meanwhile, we're putting off the meeting with the bank to discuss remortgaging the house, and we keep delaying that visit to see our parents. We overthink the unimportant and continually overlook what matters.

In a world where attention spans are waning and stress levels are surging, decision-making has never been more difficult – or more essential. And here's the thing: we have a finite amount of time and brain space reserved for making choices each day. It might sound obvious, but if we keep overthinking and obsessing about which brand of toothpaste to buy and whether to wear the grey jumper or the blue jacket, then we'll never get around to life's important decisions.

The good news is that there is a solution – a way to break free from this trap. When it comes to making decisions that matter, we have to slow down, become more intentional, and learn how to choose according to what truly matters to us. The word 'decide' originates from the Latin *decidere* (itself from *de-* 'off' + *caedere* 'cut'). It literally means 'to cut off'. What if we focused on making important decisions by focusing on our values, priorities and long-term goals, and intentionally chose to discard the rest? What if we could let go of the idea of having it *all* or making the *right* choice, and instead try to figure out what we actually want and why it's important to us?

INTRODUCTION

Once you become comfortable with the idea that no matter what you decide, there will always be something else that you could have chosen instead, you'll breathe a sigh of relief. You'll start making decisions more easily – and most importantly, you'll be happier with your final choice.

I first became interested in the topic of decision-making while preparing for a series of webinars during the Covid-19 pandemic. I'd been asked to deliver a workshop for corporate clients who had all told me similar things about their employees: that they were understandably stressed out and lacking motivation. Many of them, like me, were juggling full-time jobs as well as homeschooling their kids. It wasn't surprising that most people were re-evaluating their priorities.

I couldn't ignore the shared feeling of overwhelm, and I wanted to offer strategies, practical advice and useful tools for navigating work and life. So, I created a workshop based around three things: prioritisation, goal-setting and decision-making. After each workshop, I'd log off and immediately receive an influx of LinkedIn messages and emails from the participants. The frameworks and tools that I shared in the workshop (and now in this book) became the subject of countless enquiries and conversations. But the majority of the questions I received were about the final topic: decision-making. What I realised was that each person I spoke to – regardless of whether they were a senior leader or a junior team member, and whether they worked in marketing, finance, operations or HR – shared a need for effective decision-making tools.

In the following weeks and months, I began to experiment with different decision-making strategies. I looked at research, books and articles on the topic, and I went deep into studying the art and science of decision-making. What I learned is that our ability to make decisions is impacted by a variety of factors, from past experiences and core beliefs to societal pressure and individual bias. These factors all play a part in swaying us towards certain choices and away from others, often without us even realising it.

Life isn't a one-size-fits-all deal. Each situation, relationship and opportunity is nuanced, and therefore requires a different approach. Some decisions can be made instantly, while others require thoughtful consideration and should not be rushed. This book will help you to differentiate between the two. By creating a framework and implementing a strategic decision-making process – be it a budget, a timeline or a specific set of values-based criteria – you'll be able to minimise your options and reduce the number of choices you have to make. It might sound counterintuitive, but having constraints can be liberating. Less is more.

What I discovered from facilitating those workshops is this: while decision-making processes vary based on individual circumstances, preferences and background, there are several universal truths about decision-making that tend to apply. For instance, every choice requires trade-offs. We have to give up one thing to gain another. Understanding and accepting that we are always trading one thing in favour of something else is essential. Another example is consequences.

INTRODUCTION

Whether we like it or not, every decision has consequences, both intended and unintended. We have a responsibility to consider these outcomes before we take action. Lastly, let's not forget about context. The context surrounding the decision matters. This includes understanding why we're making the decision, how long we have in order to make it, and even who will be impacted as a result. Understanding and evaluating the unique context of each decision is crucial.

Decision-making is a skill that requires practice. All skills can be improved over time, and this is no exception. Just like refining your ability to play tennis, paint, surf or any other discipline, honing your decision-making skills involves repetition, deliberate consistent effort and learning from experience. In other words, it takes work. Sure, some people will naturally be more decisive and assertive than others, but everyone can learn how to make more effective decisions. I'm hoping that as you make your way through the chapters of this book, you'll discover a new-found sense of assurance – and that, by the end, you'll be well equipped to handle any decision-making scenario effectively. Making a choice about whether or not to spend Christmas with your parents? Trying to figure out if now is the right time to leave your job? Considering getting back together with your ex? (Okay, we all know the answer to that last one.) Anytime you're feeling stuck, overwhelmed or simply unclear about what to do, you can come back to this book, flip through its pages and revisit the strategies and models presented throughout.

There are many self-development and leadership books

written by heroes, titans and outliers. Many of them include stories about people who made it against the odds, risked it all and came out on top; they walked through fire and lived to tell the tale. This book is different. While those books are inspiring and certainly have their place, I find they often lack the nuance and real-world experience needed for navigating the complexity of life today.

Should I take financial advice from a billionaire? Sounds like a no-brainer; the logical answer is yes. But here's the thing: I'm not a billionaire, I'm a regular person. I'm trying to figure out the best way to invest £10k, not calculate the potential risk of investing millions in one deal. While a billionaire no doubt has valuable knowledge about wealth, their perspective is too far removed from my current financial reality. What I need is help from someone who understands my situation and can offer relevant and actionable advice.

I'll be real with you – I've never won an Olympic medal, never been nominated for a Nobel prize, never climbed to the summit of Mount Everest (well, not yet). I don't own a private jet, an island or a sports team. If that's what you're looking for, then this probably isn't the book for you. But the truth is that less than 0.001 per cent of people will achieve those things – or even *want* to – and yet each of us has our own goals, however big or small, and we need to make decisions every day. It's all relative. The decisions that matter to you are valid and important. This book is about decision-making for the real world. The way I see it, you don't have to become the next Bill Gates to live a happy life, have a successful career,

INTRODUCTION

maintain meaningful relationships and have a positive impact on those around you.

I did not write this book to offer life lessons and motivational quotes. Instead, what I hope to give you are insights and practical ideas that you can use to navigate decision-making in everyday life. In my work as a business advisor, board member, mentor, friend and parent, these are the strategies and processes for effective decision-making that I have tried, tested and applied to my own business and life in one way or another.

You might be reading this and thinking about the decisions you've already made throughout your life. Maybe you're reflecting on a decision that you regret, or imagining how things might be different if you'd chosen a different path. You see, the trouble with knowing whether or not we're making a 'good decision' is that it can feel as though we're trying to hit a moving target. Life is full of uncertainty, and the consequences of our choices are rarely revealed until after the fact. The benefit of hindsight means that often it's only when we look back that we gain clarity. We can see the connections, the patterns and the events that led us to making a decision. No doubt we'd probably do some things differently if we could go back in time. How many times have you thought, *Ah, if only I'd known then what I know now*, or *How was I so naive?* These are questions that can torment you, especially when facing the fallout of a decision that didn't quite pan out as you'd hoped. But it's important to remember that when you made that pivotal decision, you were not naive, and nor were you foolish. You were operating with the information, experiences and insights available to you at that moment.

Life is unpredictable, and even the most carefully calculated decisions may not always lead to the outcome we expect. But critically, when things change, we must be able to change our minds too. Our ability to adapt when circumstances change is absolutely essential. Sticking stubbornly to an initial decision when everything around us has evolved is unlikely to serve us in the long run.

Decisions, especially the ones we see as significant, are shaped by multiple factors, many of which are beyond our control. Sometimes, despite our best efforts and intentions, for one reason or another, things just don't work out. External circumstances, such as timing and even sheer luck, can influence the final outcome and there's nothing we can do about it. It's easy to label our past selves as naive, but let's exercise some compassion here and not be too hard on ourselves when we realise that we've made an unfortunate choice; hindsight has a way of casting a harsh light on past decisions.

It's equally important to remember this when everything is going well. When we get a promotion at work, when our kids succeed at school, or when we make a good investment, we're quick to pat ourselves on the back. But we're often forgetting that luck goes both ways. It's easy to fall into the trap of assuming that our success is solely a result of our effort, skill and talent – but then when we stumble and fall, when things don't go our way, we'll say it was just bad luck.

There's a Dutch saying, *Voor de wind is het goed zeilen*. This

INTRODUCTION

translates to 'Sailing is good before the wind', meaning it is easier to be successful under favourable conditions. I really like this saying, because it serves as a humbling reminder that a person's efforts alone do not result in success, and that better conditions make it much easier to succeed. In Chapter 4 we'll uncover the myriad of things we need to consider when it comes to decision-making based on our own definition of success.

Reflection serves a purpose after the fact but it doesn't really help when you're in the thick of decision-making. Practise self-compassion and humility after facing tough choices, regardless of the outcome, because you didn't know then what you know now. Limit the amount of time you spend looking back. Once a decision is made, accept that things are the way they are now, and move on.

Ever feel tempted to simply surrender all of life's decisions to fate? How much choice do you really have? Why even bother trying to figure out the 'right' decision when there are so many things to consider, so many variables, and too much uncertainty. Well, I choose to believe that you've picked up this book because deep down you understand that life is a series of choices and your choices *do* indeed matter. What I've found is that, when faced with a problem, there are two kinds of people. People who look for solutions and people who look for someone to blame. The next time you're at the train station and suddenly hear an announcement that all the trains have been cancelled, look around and you'll see this dynamic at play. Some people will complain to the rail staff, demanding to know why their journey has been delayed and who is to blame. Meanwhile, others will look around and realise, *Well, everyone's in the same boat, or rather on the same platform.* They'll ask around to see if anyone is willing to share a cab, they'll look at the local bus route – in other words, they'll find a way to solve the problem.

Throughout my life, I've always been a problem solver; the kind of person to look around and say, 'Okay, what are we going to do next?' (By 'we', I mean me, but sometimes in moments of stress I find it helpful to think in the third person. It's kind of weird, I know.) This trait became evident when I made the bold decision to pack up and leave home at the age of sixteen. After considering the worst, best and most probable outcomes of the move, it felt like an easy decision to make.

In case you were picturing an exciting, glamorous arrival, allow me to set the scene. I arrived at London Victoria coach station after spending the entire day on a bus, with nothing but a suitcase, a backpack and a Christina Aguilera poster. I had no back-up plan, no social network and no guarantee that I would find a job. But despite all of this uncertainty, I had an unwavering sense of conviction, optimism, and a stubborn self-belief that I could make it work.

This decision to venture out on my own was just the beginning. An initial leap of faith that set the stage for a series of choices that have shaped who I am today, the work that I do and the way I live my life. During those early days it would have been overwhelming to think about creating a grand master plan. Instead, I focused on making one decision at a

INTRODUCTION

time, and I tackled each challenge with a proactive mindset. I took the initiative instead of simply waiting for things to happen. A proactive mindset is about having a clear vision for where you want to go, and then rolling up your sleeves, doing the work and taking decisive action to make your ideas a reality. And you know what? It worked. Over time, my enthusiasm and tenacity opened doors to new opportunities and forged the way for a unique career and life.

I'm sure you can think of a time when you were faced with a challenging situation, yet found a way to overcome it. You didn't just give up, you kept on trying. That moment is a testament to your resilience, self-leadership and grit. When facing a difficult situation, it's easy to underestimate ourselves, forgetting the trials we've been through before and the lessons we've learned along the way. So, the next time you find yourself doubting your capabilities, don't listen to that inner critic. Remember this: you have already done hard things, you're even more capable now, and you can do it again.

Over the past two decades, I've worn many hats. I've gone from working in an Italian restaurant and fitness coaching to creating my own business, working with tech start-ups, hosting podcasts, writing books, delivering keynotes and advising global brands. These days a key part of my job is helping leaders and organisations to make strategic decisions. I've navigated various roles and industries – and like everyone else, I've encountered my fair share of obstacles.

Not many people know this, but just days before my debut book, *Power Hour*, was published, a journalist at a national newspaper wrote a scathing article about me and the book. They hadn't even read it, only glanced at the press release, yet that was enough for them to publish an article deeming the whole thing useless. Sure, I'd love to say that I shrugged it off and that it didn't bother me; an article is just one person's opinion, after all. But the truth is, at that time, I was gutted. I felt embarrassed, and what stung the most was not just their dismissal, but the fact that her words threatened to derail my entire writing career before it even really began.

Five years on, that book has sold thousands of copies, been translated into multiple languages, and received its fair share of applause and glowing reviews – but you know what? I still remember that article and the way it made me feel. Reliving that memory is almost enough to prevent me from writing another email, yet alone another book! Yet here I am.

I'm telling you this because it's easy to look at someone else's journey and think that their success came effortlessly, without criticism or a single error or stumble. We rarely get to see people's bad days – the business ideas that failed, book proposals that got rejected or investments that didn't pay off. I want you to know that it's okay to stumble, or even to fall flat on your face. It's okay to feel the sting of criticism. My mistake was not being prepared for that moment.

Looking back, it's clear that, throughout my life, every decision I've made, every risk I've taken and every challenge I've faced has played a role in shaping my career and life. Today, whether I'm developing a new business strategy, creating a detailed personal finance plan or preparing to run

INTRODUCTION

my next marathon, I rely on a set of core guiding principles and strategies to make decisions that matter. And here's the thing: so can you.

Within the chaos of our fast-paced world, decision-making requires a blend of analysis, intuition, thoughtful consideration and humility. There is a fascinating interplay between these elements, and when we learn how to combine them, not only will we make more effective decisions, but more importantly we'll be happier and more confident about the choices we've made.

As you make your way through these pages, I'd like you to actively engage with the ideas and themes. You might want to have a pen ready to highlight any words and phrases that resonate with you. Pay attention to the prompts and questions I offer – notice which ones you already have the answers for and which ones make you pause. If you're anything like me, then you'll want to share the ideas in this book with others. So, when you're done, pass it on to your partner, friend or co-worker. Talk about the decisions that have shaped their lives, how they made those choices and what they've learned along the way.

Before we race ahead into the future, let's use the lessons of the past and insights from the present to navigate the complexity of decision-making in the modern world.

1

RULES OF ENGAGEMENT

Six fundamental rules for decision-making

Netflix is known for its unique company culture, and they have several distinctive rules of engagement. One of their rules is 'no brilliant jerks'. It's a straightforward yet powerful statement that means even if someone is highly talented and skilled, their attitude matters just as much as their technical abilities. At Netflix they believe that business success often depends on the ability of team members to work together effectively. The 'no brilliant jerks' rule sends a clear message that toxic behaviour and egos are not welcome.

Beyond the walls of Netflix HQ, the concept of embracing a set of rules based on shared principles is a useful tactic. We can all benefit from applying a framework to our decision-making process. Think of rules of engagement as a set of guidelines that unofficially govern how you act and behave. Just as in a game, understanding the rules is essential.

Decision-making in the modern world can feel like navigating through a complex maze. We need a set of fundamental rules to direct us, and provide a solid foundation to fall back on in moments of doubt. Therefore, I have devised six fundamental rules of engagement specifically for making decisions that matter:

1. Determine the stakes
2. Call time
3. Make it simple
4. Send for help
5. Take no further action
6. Trust your gut

1. Determine the stakes: High, low or no

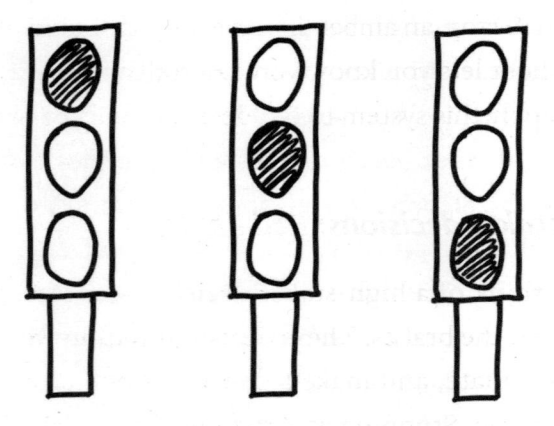

Let's begin with a relatively straightforward task: determining whether the decision is high-stakes, low-stakes or no-stakes. In other words, how significant is this decision? It's useful to picture a traffic light system. When you're driving through a busy city like Paris, London or New York, it can be pretty hectic, as there are many distractions. You've got to pay attention to other cars, weaving cyclists and people walking across the street, and follow road signs to make your way through the chaos and get to your destination. It would be almost impossible for city transportation to function without any structure or order. You might make it across the city eventually, but it would not be an easy journey.

This noisy chaotic city scene is not that dissimilar to the decision-making process that's going on inside your head in the middle of a busy day. It's necessary to build in structure to navigate your way through. So, with that in mind, let's revisit the simple but effective traffic light system. Any driver knows that as you approach a set of traffic lights, a red light means you need to stop, an amber light means you should pause and a green light lets you know you can continue. Let's see how we can apply this system to our decision-making strategy.

High-stakes decisions: Red lights

We can think of a high-stakes decision as a red light. You need to hit the brakes. These decisions require you to stop, assess, evaluate, and make a conscious choice before you can continue. Stopping at a red light in decision-making allows you to take more time, and this pause can help to prevent wrong turns and accidents. High-stakes decisions carry significant importance, substantial consequences and probably a high level of risk. The outcome can be considerable and long-lasting, so they are worthy of your time and attention.

The process designed for high-stakes decisions should include careful analysis, planning, considerable research and advice. If you're careless and make a bad choice, it could lead to setbacks, substantial loss and irreversible damage. You need to be thoughtful and take high-stakes decisions seriously.

EXAMPLES OF HIGH-STAKES DECISIONS

- Choosing to have a child
- Moving to another country
- Having a medical procedure with significant risk
- Merging or selling your business
- Taking legal action against an individual or organisation

Low-stakes decisions: Amber lights

A low-stakes decision is an amber light; it requires you to pause, take a moment to check what's going on and make sure you're going in the right direction. Low-stakes decisions require some level of consideration, but keep in mind that the outcome of your choice will have minor consequences and a relatively low level of risk. Even if you make a poor choice, it will probably lead to very little loss or gain. These kinds of decisions should not receive too much time and attention, so try to approach them with a balanced perspective. The less time you spend on low-stakes decisions, the more time you'll have for decisions that matter.

EXAMPLES OF LOW-STAKES DECISIONS

- Choosing what to watch on TV
- Picking a café for lunch with friends
- Opting for a new hairstyle
- Deciding to redecorate your bathroom
- Choosing where to sit on an empty bus

No-stakes decisions: Green lights

Lastly, let's imagine that a no-stakes decision is a green light. This requires no action at all. You have permission to proceed and continue as you were – no need for hesitation or second-guessing. Just as a green light keeps city traffic flowing, identifying a decision as no-stakes allows you to move forward confidently, knowing that the path ahead is clear.

No-stakes decisions essentially have no significant outcome or consequences at all; they are unimportant and hold no real relevance. For example, while it may seem important in the moment, the reality is that the name you choose for your pet cat doesn't have any real impact on your life. Whether you name your cat Fluffy, Ginger or Tom, it won't affect your happiness, relationships or future in any meaningful way. It's liberating to recognise that whatever you choose doesn't matter, because in the grand scheme of things it's just not that big of a deal.

> **EXAMPLES OF NO-STAKES DECISIONS**
> - Whether to sleep on the right or left side of the bed
> - Selecting a favourite flavour of ice cream
> - Putting your left shoe or right shoe on first
> - Stirring a spoon in a cup clockwise or anticlockwise
> - Deciding whether to wear your team's football shirt while watching the game, for good luck

Time can change the stakes

If you take a moment to reflect, it's likely that you have made a lot of life's high-stakes decisions already, before reading this book. Those choices have led you to the life you live today. It's human nature to imagine different scenarios, reflect on the past and contemplate the future. How many times have you thought about a past decision and wondered: *Did I make the right choice?* You see, when it comes to true high-stakes decisions, the upside is that we rarely have to make them. The downside – and the reason they require so much attention – is that they impact others as well as ourselves, and they are often hard to undo.

It's worth noting that, sometimes, low-stakes decisions can – over time and through repetition – become high-stakes. The *frequency* of a decision needs to be considered too. We make countless low-stakes decisions on a daily basis with seemingly little consequence, but when we make the same choice day after day, month after month, the effect is multiplied and those accumulated choices matter.

Take, for example, our health. We might not have had a say in our genetics, but there's no denying that the choices we make each day have a significant impact on our overall health and well-being. Most people say they would like to make time for regular exercise, opt for a well-balanced diet and practise mindfulness. Yet, for many people, maintaining a healthy lifestyle can feel like an insurmountable challenge; and it's only becoming harder as our lives get busier and the pace of life accelerates. We're bombarded with conflicting advice about which diets to choose and which exercises to do. Those tempting unhealthy foods are often within arm's reach, and every weekend provides another opportunity to have a drink or two (or three, or four).

This is one of the best examples I can provide of how the small, seemingly insignificant, choices we make today can have a profound impact over time. It's not about any single decision being inherently good or bad, but about recognising that repeatedly making the same choice will add up. The decision to take a brisk walk in the evening instead of watching another episode of a Netflix series, or selecting a banana instead of a croissant in the morning, are not in themselves life-altering choices, but when they are made repeatedly, they could lead to a much healthier, happier life.

The problem is that, all too often, we approach all of our decisions in the same way. We act as though every decision is potentially life-changing when in fact it's not. The solution: establish whether a decision is either high-stakes, low-stakes or no-stakes, and devote an appropriate amount of time and effort towards making it. All the while remembering that making the same low-stakes decision repeatedly over time can have a big impact.

2. Call time

Now let's move on to the second rule of engagement, which involves establishing how long you have to make a decision. It's critical that you allocate specific time frames for different types of decisions, especially if you find yourself contemplating the same decision over and over again without reaching a conclusion – or you've been avoiding making the decision altogether. Once you've established a reasonable time frame, be it an hour, a few days or even an entire year, you must set a final deadline to reach a conclusion. This deadline is solely for making the decision itself, not for initiating the action. For instance, if you're contemplating getting a tattoo and you've been talking about it for years but you're still unsure whether or not to get one; calling time on this means setting a deadline to decide whether or not you want to get a tattoo, rather than setting a date to get the tattoo itself.

I have a friend who's been working on his passion project on and off for years. He's a teacher but he's also written three children's books. In the past, we've talked about him pitching the books to publishers, and a few years ago he started a social media account and bought a web domain address – but he never posts, and he's yet to launch the website. He's told me countless times that even though he enjoys his work as a teacher, he's envious of his entrepreneurial friends – people who don't work a nine-to-five job, people who are creating their own work, people like me. He assures me that he is going to publish his books one day, but it never seems to be the right time. He's too busy, he needs a bit more money, he's not quite ready.

If you're procrastinating over a decision like this and find yourself delaying the launch of your podcast/not signing up for the marathon/avoiding sharing your artwork, perhaps you need to interrogate the reason for your procrastination. Ask yourself: *Do I really want to do this? Why am I putting it off? If not now, then when? Do I really need more time, more preparation, more advice before I can start?*

Questions like these are confronting and can be uncomfortable, but if you take the time to answer them, you'll find the true reason for your avoidance. Few people are willing to answer these kinds of questions, as it's much easier to brush them off with excuses or distractions. But facing them head-on is the only way to break through the barrier of procrastination. And when you do ask yourself these questions – and force yourself to answer them – you open the door to possibility.

If you make the decision to start today, what could be different one year from now? The thing about time is that it passes regardless of our decisions. Setting a time frame for making decisions is invaluable, because it creates a sense of urgency and accountability – a deadline serves as a catalyst for action.

High-impact decisions, such as moving house or changing jobs, may require a lot of time to make. You will likely need to spend a few weeks researching, planning or getting advice from somebody else. Block out some space in your schedule to meet with a friend or mentor to discuss your dilemma. Even if you're making the decision without any external input, you should still block out some focused time to make this important decision before a set deadline. The fast pace of modern life means we're often too 'busy' and so have very little time for contemplation. Think of the red light, hit the brakes and make an assessment before you continue.

You might be wondering when the best time is to make a decision. A study published in the journal *Cognition* showed that the most accurate decision-making happens earlier on in the day between 8 a.m. and 1 p.m. Throughout the day, our energy is being depleted both physically and mentally. We've all been there – staring blankly at a screen, feeling drained after hours of thinking, problem-solving and mental gymnastics. As the day carries on, we're more likely to commit errors, forget important information and make poor choices. The morning is when we typically make the most accurate and thoughtful decisions, and we tend to be more cautious and meticulous. We hit an energy plateau in the afternoon, and by evening our decision-making may be more erratic. It seems obvious but worth repeating that we should avoid making any high-stakes decisions when we're overly tired or hungry.

'Decision fatigue' is a well-documented phenomenon that describes the mental and emotional exhaustion that occurs as we navigate through a multitude of choices throughout the day. You see, every time we make a decision – whether it's ordering a coffee or devising a new strategy at work – our finite mental resources are being depleted. Research has shown that the human brain has a limited capacity for making decisions, and so the more choices we make, the more our ability to make sound judgements diminishes.

For example, a study published in *The Proceedings of the National Academy of Sciences* found that judges were more likely to grant parole to prisoners earlier in the day, when their mental energy was highest, and less likely to do so as the day progressed and decision fatigue set in. After analysing more than 1,100 parole decisions over a year, the researchers found that the timing of the hearing was the primary indicator of parole approval. Prisoners who had earlier scheduled appointments received parole in around 70 per cent of cases, whereas prisoners with later hearings were granted parole in around 10 per cent fewer cases. Researchers stated that 'as the day progresses, decision fatigue influences the decision of the judges more'. This illustrates how decision fatigue can have real-world consequences.

It's as if we have an energy budget for decision-making, and with each choice, we're spending a little bit more of that allowance. Decision fatigue cannot differentiate between the monumental and the mundane. So be mindful when you're planning your schedule and checking things off your to-do list. If your aim is to be more productive and more decisive, start with the most difficult things first, and leave the easier (and probably more enjoyable) tasks until later.

Consider both your physical and your emotional energy. If you've had a busy day at work, spent an hour stuck in traffic or haven't had dinner yet, and suddenly start thinking about a potentially life-altering decision, acknowledge that this is not the best time for you to think clearly and to problem-solve. Temporarily postpone making any high-stakes decisions that you might later regret, and instead take a look at your diary and plan a meeting with yourself. Don't worry, this doesn't have to be as formal as it sounds. It could be an early morning walk around the block or a bike ride through the park. The key is to make sure that the time is dedicated to making the important decision. It's impossible to know with 100 per cent certainty that you've made the right choice, of course, but if you take the time you need then you will reach a conclusion one way or another.

Now comes the tough part: committing to your decision.

RULES OF ENGAGEMENT

Being willing to commit to a decision takes courage, a little bit of optimism and acceptance. Sometimes after making a high-stakes decision such as selling a house or initiating a break-up, it's natural to start second-guessing yourself. That's completely normal. It doesn't necessarily mean you've made the wrong choice; it means you're experiencing a reaction that psychologists call 'post-decisional dissonance'. In other words, you freak out and your mind starts throwing up all sorts of questions and confusing thoughts. This happens because, when you're dealing with a high-stakes decision, it's likely that there's going to be some change and uncertainty, leading you to feel anxious and unsure. The good news is that these feelings are temporary, and will typically lessen as you adjust to the new situation.

When you start to question your decision, don't overreact – take a minute to remind yourself of the reasons you made that choice in the first place. In the modern world, commitment seems to be increasingly rare. With so many options available, it's easy to jump from one thing to another, never fully committing to anything. But as I see it, commitment isn't something to fear, it's something to embrace. When you commit, you're not just making a decision, you're making a statement about what you stand for. Think about it: every remarkable achievement, meaningful relationship and decision that matters requires commitment.

Committing doesn't mean you just stick to your decision, with a fixed mindset, unable to ever change your view. Rather, it means having conviction and believing that, after thoughtful consideration, you made the best choice according to the information you had at the time. So, be bold and remember that anything you have chosen is worthy of commitment.

What about seemingly trivial decisions, such as selecting what to wear to work each day? Several well-known people have chosen to wear the same clothes daily to minimise decision-making and streamline their lives. During his presidency, Barack Obama was known to wear only grey or blue suits. In an interview with *Vanity Fair*, he mentioned that he did this intentionally, stating that he didn't want to make decisions about what to wear because he had too many other decisions to make. Steve Jobs, the late co-founder of Apple, was famous for his signature black turtleneck, blue jeans, and sneakers. And Matilda Kahl, an art director from New York, wears a 'uniform' of a white silk shirt and black trousers to work every day, to alleviate the daily stress and time spent deciding what to wear.

I'm not suggesting that we all adopt this approach. However, I would suggest giving yourself a fixed amount of time to make your choice (set a timer for ten minutes, or however long you have given yourself) – and then, when the time is up, pick one and move on. Low-stakes decisions require strict time limits, or you can easily waste a lot of time and energy overthinking them. Trust me, this might just change your life. If you're not convinced, try to remember the last singular low-stakes decision you made that had profound and lasting consequences. Can you even remember what you ate for dinner last Friday night? I rest my case.

Calling time on a decision is also important when you're

trying to problem-solve as part of a group. Think of the last time you tried to arrange a dinner with friends, and had to face the dreaded WhatsApp group chat dilemma. Typically, the thread goes on and on, you have to read hundreds of messages, and you all spend far too long in a limbo state of indecision before a restaurant reservation is made, if one gets made at all. Next time this happens, instead of asking everyone in the group to suggest a date, time and place to meet – throwing way too many options into the mix – lead the group's decision-making by trying something like this:

> Hi, I'd really love to see you all. Let's catch up over dinner. I've reserved a table for the 4 of us at my favourite Japanese restaurant, next Friday at 8pm [insert restaurant name and address].
>
> Please let me know if you can make it? If I don't hear from you by tomorrow, I'll assume you can't make it and adjust the reservation.
>
> PS The cocktails are exceptional! Hope to see you there.

It's likely that most people in the group will respond to the message within a day. Try it, and see for yourself. Being clear about your time frame prompts people to make a decision and respond. If they're busy making lots of decisions themselves, they'll probably be grateful that you've taken the initiative to make a reservation for a set time and place, and now all they have to do is turn up. It's a win for everyone.

Timing matters in more ways than one, so add these strategies to your toolkit to use as and when required. Setting a deadline will help you to overcome procrastination and reach a conclusion one way or another. Making decisions in the early hours, rather than at the end of the day, is likely to lead to better outcomes. It's natural to have doubts, but this doesn't mean you've made a poor choice. Once you make up your mind, be brave enough to commit to your decision. Lastly, in a group setting, you will save time and unnecessary deliberation by taking the lead and steering the group towards decisive action.

3. Make it simple

Have you ever tried to select a holiday destination, plan a travel itinerary and stick to a budget? Initially, it's fun. You grab your laptop and begin to search online for ideas and inspiration. First on the list is a beautiful beach resort in Greece; it looks like the perfect place to rest and relax. But wait, you really like the idea of exploring a city with an interesting history and vibrant culture – maybe somewhere like Prague. However, an adrenaline-fuelled adventure would be fun, so how about a hiking trip in the Austrian Alps? Or maybe something a bit more fun, like a music festival or weekend in Ibiza? Perhaps you don't need to go abroad – the Cornish coast looks idyllic!

But the weather might not be so good. Okay, so how about a cold-weather trip? What about skiing? Or snowboarding? You could invite some friends and arrange a group trip, but ideally you want to spend some time with your partner as a couple. Rome, the city of romance – that's a good option!

It's not long before you're feeling overwhelmed by this seemingly unending task. Planning a holiday is supposed to be fun, but the long list of city breaks, beach resorts, adventure trails and campsites is impossible to choose from. The choices are endless!

This kind of situation – which can occur when choosing your next holiday, buying a new laptop or searching for a new podcast to listen to – is known as 'analysis paralysis'. While decision fatigue occurs when there are too *many* decisions to make, analysis paralysis happens when there are so many options and variables to consider for just one decision that it becomes overwhelming. You find it hard to make a decision, or take any action at all. This state of over-analysis is stressful and ultimately makes it almost impossible to know if you're making the right choice. For instance, imagine I ask you to bring a bottle of olive oil to a dinner party. A pretty simple task, right? If you walk into a shop with only two types of olive oil, making a choice is easy. But what if the shop offers thirty different kinds? Suddenly the decision becomes much more complicated. You might start comparing costs, sizes, flavours, organic versus non-organic, extra-virgin versus virgin, and so on. It's overwhelming, and suddenly all those options mean you're unable to decide and you show up to the party empty-handed.

It's bad enough if you're attempting to make this decision alone, but analysis paralysis is even worse if two or more people have to agree on the same decision. I guess this is why so many couples find themselves arguing in the middle of IKEA while trying to decide which bedside lamp to buy. The sheer number of options can lead to a heated debate about style preferences, practicality, budget, and whether or not you even need a lamp in the first place. (See the first rule above: determine the stakes. It's important to define the type of decision you're making so you know how to approach it and how much time it really deserves.)

Whether you're planning a holiday or buying a lamp, you have to overcome analysis paralysis in order to take action. A smart way to tackle overthinking is to simplify and reduce the number of viable options. This technique is particularly useful when you're feeling overwhelmed by the abundance of choice. Narrow it down, be ruthless and you'll save yourself a lot of time. There are many ways to do this, but here is one effective method that I often use myself:

PROCESS OF ELIMINATION

Grab a piece of paper and write a list of the most realistic and viable options. This doesn't have to be in any specific order. Let's use the holiday example again:

- Beach resort – Greece
- City break – Prague
- Hiking – Austria
- Party – Ibiza
- Staycation – Cornwall
- Skiing / snowboarding – France
- Group trip – Unknown destination
- Romantic trip – Rome

Now, select two options and compare them before permanently eliminating one. For example: a city break in Prague versus a staycation in Cornwall. State a reason for your choice, and then cross the other option off the list. Let's say you select Prague because you've never been there before and you have already been to Cornwall many times. Done. Cornwall is now eliminated. Don't spend too long agonising over each one – be ruthless. If you get stuck, call time in order to reach a definitive outcome. Repeat this process until eventually you have only two remaining options and then make your final choice.

Whenever I use the process of elimination technique, I pretty much always feel satisfied with my final choice. If you get to the end of all that work and you're still unsure, try to step back and get some perspective. When it comes to life's many problems, selecting a holiday destination is a pretty good one to have to solve. Plus, it's helpful to remember that you'll likely make a choice like this again in future. By making a selection you are not necessarily eliminating all other options forever – just for now.

4. Send for help

Moving on to the fourth rule of engagement: send for help. It's okay to admit it: making significant decisions can be intimidating, especially if it feels like you're carrying the weight of the decision on your own. Asking for help is not only acceptable but often beneficial. Sometimes, we get wrapped up in our own heads, and emotions can cloud our judgement. Seeking advice from other people can offer a fresh, impartial viewpoint, to help us see things more clearly. Today we might call it 'crowdsourcing', but our ancestors called it the 'wisdom of the tribe'. Fundamentally, the concept remains the same: just as our ancestors relied on the collective knowledge, experiences and traditions of their community to navigate life's challenges, we can gather ideas and collect advice from a diverse group to solve a problem together.

If you're lucky, you'll have some trusted friends, family members or mentors who are willing to give you objective feedback, make you aware of potential blind spots and call you out on your nonsense. We all need people who are willing to tell us the truth and tell us when we are wrong – even when it's hard to hear. Kim Scott, leadership coach and author of *Radical Candor*, states in her book that 'Nobody really wants to hear criticism. Focus on the fact that you can only fix problems you know about and that if the person cares enough to make you aware of a problem, they might also help you fix it.'

That said, not all advice is created equal, so it's wise to be selective about who you turn to for guidance. Seek out people who've been in a similar situation before and ask yourself: *Do they have relevant experience or expertise in the matter? Do they have a track record of making good decisions – or have they learned lessons from the bad ones?* Either way, if they have more experience than you, it's likely they are the wiser for it.

Listen to people who want more for you, not more from you. People you trust to provide constructive criticism as well as positive feedback. Those who know you well and have your best interests at heart. And use feedback gained from others as one input in your decision-making process, making sure to weigh it up against your own judgement. Remember that while seeking advice is valuable, it's not a quick-fix solution. You cannot relinquish all responsibility and blindly follow the suggestions of others. Ultimately, the final decision still rests with you.

In the world of work, many of us have embraced the idea of collaboration and teamwork. Most organisations have more than one person working on a particular project, and assemble a team with different skills and varied perspectives. Each team member knows their role and what they are responsible for. Together, they are able to get more work done, come up with better ideas and support each other. This typically makes work easier and more enjoyable. Any good leader knows that they cannot do everything by themselves, and so they learn to delegate certain tasks and decisions to other people.

I recently worked with a start-up founder who came to me for advice. She told me that after almost two years of working on her business, she was frustrated, exhausted and making little progress. I asked her about the company's business plan, key objectives and team dynamics. Immediately I realised that she was attempting to do the work of four people by herself. My advice was this: picture yourself trying to play a football match against a team of eleven players, all by yourself. No matter how hard you try, how fast you run or how skilled you are, your chances of winning are virtually zero. You can't do the work of the goalkeeper, defenders and striker all at the same time.

Sometimes we need to work with others, and be part of a team that can help us to achieve success. And why limit this approach solely to work? There's merit in applying it to our personal lives too. I'll admit, this one takes some getting used to, and it's something I struggle with myself. But delegating decisions and sharing the workload will save you a lot of time and energy, as well as empowering others around you to take the lead. Initially it might be hard to let go of control – but trust me, it's a necessary step in the decision-making process.

RULES OF ENGAGEMENT

When you're organising a party for friends or family, such as a birthday, baby shower or Christmas dinner, don't feel like it needs to all be on you. Delegate by assigning different aspects of the event – such as booking a venue, planning an activity, organising the catering and drinks – to various people in the group. This not only shares the responsibility, but also allows others to bring their ideas and creativity to the table. It means you can provide general guidelines and oversee the process without getting bogged down in every detail.

It's worth remembering that effective delegation requires communication and trust, so start off by asking everyone if and how they would like to contribute, then try to assign the right task to the right person by playing to each person's unique strengths. Make sure they understand the guidelines and expectations, then allow them to play their part. It might feel uncomfortable at first, especially if you're used to doing things alone. (First-born daughters, I'm looking at you.) Relying on others requires trust and a little bit of optimism. But remember: by delegating decisions, you not only lighten your own load but also give others the opportunity to develop their skills and confidence.

In the end, it's about realising that you don't have to bear the weight of every decision alone. None of us has all the answers – I don't; you don't; even your parents, despite what they might say, don't know everything. So take some time to gather advice from a diverse group, lean into collaboration, and master the art of delegation. In doing so, it's likely you'll achieve better outcomes and empower others along the way.

5. Take no further action

Next, let's address a fundamental aspect of decision-making: whether to take action or not. Let me be clear – inaction is not the same as *choosing* not to act. They might appear the same on the surface, but there is a subtle and important difference.

Inaction is what happens when we passively let time slip away, allowing circumstances to go unchanged. It can be driven by fear or an attempt to avoid discomfort. While it's mostly unconscious, it is still a choice – one that often leads to missed opportunities. We've all heard the phrase 'missed the boat' – a concept that perfectly illustrates the brutal reality of indecision and inaction.

In contrast, making a deliberate decision to do nothing is a conscious choice. There are many situations when taking action is necessary, but there will be instances where doing nothing could lead to a better outcome in the end. For example, some parents can be tempted to help their children with day-to-day tasks such as preparing breakfast, tying their shoelaces and packing a bag for school. Although well intended, these efforts to help can be misplaced. Some parents want to get everything done quickly and with as little mess as possible, so they will repeatedly step in and assist. However, as I've learned, the simple act of allowing children to do some things by themselves, and to make mistakes and learn from them, can enhance their development, self-confidence and growth. As children get older, if given the chance to make

Inaction is not the same as *choosing* not to act

their own choices, they learn how to assess situations, make decisions, and take responsibility for the consequences of their actions. This independence is crucial for their future self-sufficiency.

I remember one Sunday morning when my son and I were getting ready to go to his weekly football match. Usually, I would ask him to pack his bag and then I'd check to see that he'd packed his football boots, gloves and a drink, but this time I decided to take a step back. Just as we were walking out of the house, I asked him if he had everything he needed; without much consideration, he responded with a 'yes'. I paused for a moment and glanced back into the hallway to see his football boots on the floor by the coat stand. 'Alright, let's go,' I said, closing the front door.

When we arrived at the pitch, I watched as he rummaged around in his bag trying to locate his boots. Then he looked up and said, 'Mum, I can't find my football boots, they're not in my bag.' With only a few minutes to go before the start of the match, there wasn't enough time to go get them, so we asked the coach and other parents to see if anyone could help. One of his teammates had a spare pair of boots, but they were one size too small for him. So now he had two options: he could either wear a pair of uncomfortable shoes and play, or forgo the match and watch from the sidelines. He chose to squeeze his feet into the boots and play.

I'll admit I did feel a little guilty, but I wanted him to learn an important lesson. The following Sunday morning, he was clutching his football boots as we walked out of the house.

Lesson learned? I'd love to say that I never had to check his bag again and that he never forgot his boots after that, but if you're a parent you'll know that's not how the story goes. However, it was an important step in the right direction for him, and a good lesson for me that doing nothing can sometimes be the right decision.

The same principle applies for business leaders, coaches and managers too. One of the best things we can do as a leader is provide opportunities for others to learn and develop. When we take a step back, not only does it demonstrate that we trust others and have confidence in their ability to make good decisions, it also gives them an opportunity to find solutions that we might not have thought of ourselves. Even when spotting a potential error or preventable mistake, the choice to take no action at all can still be the best decision. Allow people to figure things out on their own and make decisions independently.

Let's examine how this idea applies to your personal relationships and interactions. Consider the decision to speak, criticise or complain about something trivial. Is it likely to lead to a good outcome? Is there a better time to have this conversation? If you're feeling tired, stressed or distracted, it's probably better to wait for a more opportune moment. Ask yourself: *Does this really matter – and if it matters, is this the best time to tackle the issue?* Sometimes the best thing we can do in the moment is nothing at all.

Remember, this isn't the same as inaction, turning a blind eye or ignoring issues; it's about recognising that not every minor situation or problem needs immediate attention. Is this a low-stakes or no-stakes scenario? Knowing when to be silent and when to speak up is an art in itself, and making a conscious choice about when and where to invest your time and energy isn't always easy. Nevertheless, it's a choice that can make all the difference in the world.

6. Trust your gut

> 'Intuition is thinking that you know without knowing why you do'
>
> – Daniel Kahneman

When reason and logic fall short, a crucial element that is often overlooked is your intuition. While there are times when it's crucial to analyse and assess a situation, don't underestimate the value of instinct. If something instantly feels right or wrong, that reaction is worth further examination.

How many times have you heard the advice 'trust your gut'? I've heard it said countless times by coaches, teachers, business mentors, therapists and spiritual gurus. It's a relatively simple instruction, but that doesn't mean it's easy to put into practice. What exactly does it mean to trust your gut, and when should you heed this advice? Most of us have never been taught how to identify when our intuition is sounding alarm bells or how to use this powerful tool when making decisions.

And what exactly is intuition? Well, it's more than just a feeling or a nagging voice telling you to hold back or urging you to jump in. Intuition, often likened to pattern recognition, plays a pivotal role in decision-making. It functions by allowing our brains to quickly and effectively process vast amounts of information, by spotting familiar patterns based on past experiences and learned associations. While analysis has its place, there are moments when intuition can offer a shortcut to clarity. It's that inexplicable certainty – the feeling deep within that tells you what's right.

For instance, when an experienced doctor meets a new patient, they're often looking for patterns in symptoms and behaviour to make a diagnosis. Let's say the doctor is presented with a baby exhibiting a fever and small red spots and blisters on their face and body. They may ask the parents some questions, but at the same time the doctor's intuition is working too. Years of medical training and countless encounters with babies showing similar symptoms have taught the doctor to recognise the pattern almost instinctively. They have seen this scenario play out time and time again, and each repetition adds another data point to their mental database – a sort of subconscious tally chart. So, when the doctor looks at that baby, intuition kicks in and suggests that the baby most probably has chickenpox. This happens quickly, as they recognise all the symptoms and start to connect the dots (no pun intended). It's not magic, or a hunch. The doctor isn't a genius. Their instinct is the result of seeing hundreds or even thousands of similar cases before, refining their ability to make a split-second diagnosis based on patterns they've seen in the past.

Our ability to spot patterns and react quickly plays out in other ways too. In the world of sports, split-second decisions can make or break a match. Imagine a tennis player battling through an intense rally. Each time their opponent hits the ball, they have a split second to respond and return the ball. There's no time to consciously weigh up the angle, speed and spin of the ball consciously. Instead, intuition takes over, honed through years of practice and countless repetitions of hitting the ball. A player who has hit 10,000 shots has created a mental library of patterns and scenarios, so they know instinctively what to do. They know when to hit forehand, backhand, volley; when to move closer to the net and when to hold back. It's not luck that makes them elite players, it's the combination of muscle memory, instinct and pattern recognition, finely tuned through years of practice.

Just as intuition can help us make split-second decisions based on familiar patterns, it can also serve as a warning – a cautionary alarm – letting us know that something is potentially dangerous. Whether it's on a first date, during a business negotiation or just an everyday situation such as noticing that the milk smells bad, our ability to spot patterns that are indicative of trouble ahead is commonly referred to as 'seeing red flags'. It's that feeling of recognising that something isn't quite right. It might be a series of subtle cues that you've seen before, hinting at some underlying issues, or just a general feeling of discomfort and unease. When we pay attention to red flags, it allows us to pre-emptively course-correct. In other words, we can avoid walking into avoidable pitfalls.

By leveraging pattern recognition, you can take a proactive approach to decision-making. So, next time your intuition sends up a red flag, don't ignore it; it's a canary in the coal mine – an early indicator that something's not right.

Daniel Kahneman was a world-famous scientist, psychologist and winner of the Nobel Prize in Economics, best known for his work on the psychology of judgement and decision-making. His book *Thinking, Fast and Slow* introduces the dual process theory, and explains how intuition and reasoning shape our judgement and influence the decisions we make. As he describes it, when we're making decisions, there are two different systems of thinking. System 1 is our intuition or gut feeling, based on past experiences and repetition: it's fast, automatic, emotional and mostly subconscious. System 2 is slower and more deliberate: it involves consciously working through different considerations, applying different strategies and concepts, and weighing them all up.

To understand how this theory plays out in our daily lives, consider the following situation. Imagine leaving home in the early hours of the morning to commute from home to work. It's the same journey you've made hundreds of times before, so requires a relatively low level of thought. System 1 dominates in this familiar scenario because you know where you're going, how long it's going to take and what to expect, based on previous experience. You can operate in a sort of cognitive cruise control, using very little energy and not thinking too much.

Now, let's consider an alternative situation. You've just

arrived at JFK airport to visit New York City for the first time. After seeing the long queue at the taxi rank, you decide to take the subway instead. You check the subway map, figure out the right route, and estimate how long it will take to make your way across the city to arrive at your hotel. Being in a new place means you need to stop and think. You need to pay attention and make conscious choices. This is when system 2 – deliberate thinking and reasoning – kicks into gear. Kahneman suggests that even though system 1 usually guides our initial impressions, system 2 then steps in to provide deeper analysis. Often, we're using *both* systems when making decisions.

You may be wondering how to know when to trust intuition, and when to take a more analytical approach. It's a valid question, and the key is to find a delicate balance between the two. Intuition and logic are not rivals; they are complementary forces. They each offer useful insights that can guide you towards making an effective choice.

This interplay between intuition and analysis is complex – and like many things in life, there isn't a universal problem-solving hack to apply to any and all decisions. The best thing we can do is pay attention to our gut feeling, remembering that it serves a purpose and is there for a reason. When intuition alone is not enough, the next step is deeper interrogation and thoughtful analysis. By striking a balance, and combining both, it's possible to have the best of both worlds; to trust our gut feeling and then investigate further with logical reasoning.

RULES OF ENGAGEMENT

So, there you have it. A decision-making manifesto. Six simple but effective rules of engagement to keep in mind as you make your way through the various themes laid out in this book.

Determine the stakes

Call time

Make it simple

Send for help

Take no further action

Trust your gut

Disclaimer: You don't have to wait until you've read the entire book to start implementing these strategies. Think about it: are there any upcoming decisions that could benefit from a more structured approach – such as setting clear time limits or eliminating some options from the table? Challenge yourself to implement at least one new strategy in your decision-making toolkit this week, and observe how it impacts the outcome. Remember to keep the rules of engagement in your back pocket to be used whenever necessary.

2

VALUES

Value-led decision-making, balancing competing values, creating a rule book

My son and I love watching movies together, and recently I've been introducing him to some old favourites from my youth – ones I watched repeatedly when I was a kid. The list includes *Cool Runnings*, *Jumanji*, *Sister Act* and *Space Jam*. I've seen these films countless times, but rewatching them twenty years later reminds me of the enduring power of storytelling.

Our latest movie choice was *The Mighty Ducks* – a sports comedy released in 1992. It's a story about a high-flying lawyer called Gordon Bombay, who is forced to coach a youth ice hockey team as part of his community service. Initially he is uninterested and reluctant to coach this team of misfits, but as the story unfolds, Gordon rediscovers his love for the game and teaches the kids about teamwork, perseverance and the importance of friendship. There's a pivotal scene where Charlie, a key player on the Ducks team, faces a moral dilemma. During a crucial game, the coach is pressuring him to fake an injury, to cheat in order to help the Ducks score a goal. Despite the pressure and the potential short-term gain for the team, when the moment comes Charlie stays true to his principles and refuses to cheat. It's a powerful moment, and his decision underscores the film's theme of integrity and choosing to do what's right over taking shortcuts to success.

Even though Charlie is only twelve years old (and a fictional character), his choice to play fairly demonstrates a salient lesson in the importance of aligning our actions with our personal values, no matter the circumstances. Watching this movie while sitting beside my son got me thinking. How do our values change throughout our lives? As we get older, do we tend to lose sight of them? How do we discover what our values are in the first place? When and why do we forsake them, and how important are they in decision-making?

As we navigate decisions in our lives – big or small, high-stakes or low-stakes – the importance of understanding our personal values cannot be overstated. Our values are what we care about most deeply and what we stand for, and they influence how we act and behave. Even if you've never spent time considering what your values are, they will have played a part in shaping you and steered you to where you are today. When making decisions, our values can serve as a compass and keep us moving in the right direction. Once we truly understand what they are, our values can become a foundation on which to build our character and reputation.

It's not enough to merely recite our values as though they have been written for us; we must live by them. Our core values should act as checkpoints for every aspect of our lives, from the everyday small stuff to the defining moments. This is what's known as 'value-led decision-making'. This involves aligning our choices and actions with what we consider to be important and what we believe is morally right. As we will explore in this chapter, it also requires us to find a balance between conflicting values – prioritising those that are most essential and relevant to each situation. This is inevitably going to involve trade-offs and compromise.

With that said, although our values may stay the same throughout our lives, it's likely that the hierarchy of their importance will change. Life is not static, and at each different stage, our circumstances, commitments and priorities will undoubtedly shift too.

Ultimately, our values not only define who we are but who we aspire to be. Understanding how they can influence our decisions is an ongoing process that requires considerable thought and self-reflection, and it's one that is probably going to feel uncomfortable and challenging at times. But trust me, doing this sort of work consistently will pay off down the line. Knowing what your values are can provide you with an emotional anchor and a framework to make decisions that allow you to construct a life that is meaningful, a life that you enjoy living – a life that you chose.

What do you value the most?

So, how do you start to make value-led decisions? The first step is to uncover what your values are, followed by their order of priority. If this feels a bit overwhelming and you're not sure where to start, I have a process that can help. Find a quiet corner, get yourself a cup of coffee, and make sure you're sitting comfortably. Reflect for a moment on your own life experiences, upbringing, influences and role models, and you'll no doubt spot some patterns and common themes. What kind of home did you grow up in, and what mattered to you and everyone else around you? Was there a moment in your life when you realised that something was significant and important to you? These questions can help you to identify core themes.

If you grew up in a house filled with music and art, you may value creativity. If your parents were strict and encouraged you to always adhere to rules, you might rebel against authority and value autonomy. It's likely that you value many things, such as adventure, family, health and freedom. They're all important, each for a different reason, but it's helpful to identify which are the *most* important to you at this moment in your life.

If you're still unsure about what your values are and how they rank in order of importance, here are some more prompts to help you with identifying and defining them:

- Think about people you admire and respect. What is it about them that inspires you? What values and qualities do they represent?

VALUES

....

....

....

....

- On the other side of the coin, when you think about people that you do not like or respect, what qualities do they share that are unappealing to you?

....

....

....

....

- What makes you angry? What makes you excited? When something elicits a strong emotional response it's a signpost that it is related to something important to you.

DECISIONS THAT MATTER

....

....

....

....

Our daily actions and habits shine a light onto the things we value. For example, a person who values their well-being will engage in regular physical activity, mindful practices and eat healthily. A person who values freedom and autonomy might choose to work for themselves or remain single. The truth is, every day you make choices and decisions that reflect what you value. Just take a look at your schedule for the past year. How did you spend your time? Who did you spend it with? Did you reschedule a meeting with your co-workers because it clashed with your daughter's karate presentation? Have you spent the last four Saturdays hungover and unable to go to that yoga class? You'll go next week, right? You get the point. What I'm trying to highlight is the fact that our consistent actions, even the small ones, indicate what we are choosing to value the most.

I did warn you that uncovering your values can be an

uncomfortable process. You have to be honest with yourself and look at your current reality: are the things you're doing each day going to make you the person/parent/partner/leader that you want to be? Are you aligning your actions with your intentions? When you have a clear understanding of what matters most to you, it becomes easier to prioritise your values and for these to be reflected in the decisions you make.

For instance, if creativity is high-value for you, think of at least three practical actions you could take to ensure it is central to your life. For example:

1. Designate a space in your home or office that inspires creative work.

2. Schedule regular time in your weekly routine dedicated solely to engaging in creative activities and hobbies.

3. Sign up to a new learning opportunity, such as an online workshop or course that can introduce you to new ways of thinking.

Remember, nobody can tell you if your values are right or wrong. Only you know what is meaningful for you and why you value the things you do.

Understanding where your values come from

As much as we might like to think we are making decisions independently and forging our own path, many of our underlying beliefs and assumptions are ingrained within us like strands of cultural DNA, inherited from our parents and grandparents. It's important to examine which values you may have selected for yourself, and which you might have inherited.

We're often quick to point to genetics as the reason for our freckles, hay fever and fear of spiders, but we might not recognise that some of our behaviours and beliefs are inherited too. The stories you heard around the table growing up may seem redundant and irrelevant to your current situation – however, other people's values have impacted and influenced yours. Your family's values, religious views, politics and culture have all played a part in shaping your thoughts and behaviours today. By examining the principles you have inherited, you can separate them into those you choose to discard and those you choose to keep.

I have a friend who was born and raised in Japan, but has lived here in the UK for the last twenty years. I first met her ten years ago – our sons became friends at nursery, and are still good friends to this day. Whenever I am meeting her I do my best to arrive early because I know how much she values punctuality. One day I was ten minutes late for our lunch meeting. She was upset and explained that, in Japanese culture, lateness is rude and disrespectful as it implies that you don't appreciate the other person's time, or that their time is less important than yours. Punctuality is highly valued, and everyone is expected to be on time for meetings and appointments.

I apologised of course, but initially felt that her reaction was a little bit over the top. It was only ten minutes, and amongst my other friends that was socially acceptable. Travelling with a three-year-old means you can pretty much guarantee that twenty minutes into any car journey, they'll announce that they immediately need to go to the toilet and you'll be forced to make a detour. But irrespective of the reason, I could see how much she was bothered by my lateness so I agreed to try my best to be on time in the future.

A few weeks later, she told me that she was going to try to be more flexible, in an attempt to accommodate my culture of acceptable lateness. She said, 'I am Japanese, but I am no longer in Japan.' Turns out I wasn't her only Western friend who'd arrived late to lunch. Although this might seem like a relatively small issue, it highlights how our values can impact our actions, ideas and relationships. After we talked, we both understood that, despite our cultural differences, we cherished our friendship enough to meet each other halfway. Our connection was preserved through compromise and a mutual understanding of the values most important to us, as friends and individuals.

However, it's worth noting that, sometimes, the gap is too vast to bridge and it's not possible to reconcile differing values. For example, if one person values honesty above all else and another views dishonesty as an acceptable tool in certain situations, it can lead to conflicts that are difficult or even impossible to resolve. When our core values are deeply tied to religious or moral beliefs it can be even harder – and sometimes, despite our best intentions, we have to accept that not every relationship can withstand fundamental differences. In moments like this, integrity and courage are needed to make tough choices, even when it is uncomfortable or feels inconvenient. Ultimately, what matters most is knowing that we're being authentic and making decisions that are aligned with our personal values.

How emotions impact decision-making

Sometimes we forget about our values and make impulsive decisions. Unlike value-led decisions, impulsive decisions are often led by emotions – and they don't always deliver the best outcomes. When we're feeling overly excited, it's likely we'll say 'yes' without hesitation. However, when we're annoyed or angry we're more likely to say 'no' to the same request. Have you ever sent an angry email, then a few hours later wished that you hadn't? Have you got so carried away in the excitement of planning a holiday with friends that you agreed to a trip that you couldn't really afford?

We all make emotion-led decisions sometimes, but when this happens it's important to ask yourself *when*, *why* and *for whom* you acted so quickly. Try to remember the last time you made an impulsive, emotion-led decision. How did you feel at that moment? What was the final outcome? If you could go back, would you do it again? As well as being led by emotions, we might also forget to consider our values when we're forced to make decisions under pressure. Marketers tell us to act quickly, buy now and book your tickets today! You must seize the moment before it's too late, or potentially miss out on an incredible opportunity or a limited-time offer. The reason this tactic works so well is because it taps into our emotional brain and guides us to make an emotion-led decision. We don't want to be left standing at the harbour watching the boat sail away. This leaves very little time for critical thinking or analysis – we have to act now and think later.

When you feel as though you're under pressure to make a quick decision, whether it's about taking a new job, selling your home or signing up for a hiking holiday, stop and consider the following: *Is this decision urgent, or is it important?* Urgent situations require immediate action. If you've been in a real emergency, then you'll know you have to act fast without any thought at all. System 1, intuitive action, kicks in. When the house is on fire, your ability to make quick decisions without overthinking is crucial. But if you're lucky, most decisions will not require such a rapid response. When you feel as though you need time to make up your mind and the situation allows for it, do not let unnecessary urgency – or pressure from others – influence the outcome of your decision. If it's urgent, act fast. If it's important, take your time.

Urgent | Important

Are you living in alignment with your values?

Even if you're not 100 per cent certain you're making value-led decisions, you'll certainly know if your actions are *not* in alignment with your values. It's a feeling that is hard to describe, but easy to recognise. Sometimes, you will find yourself in situations where your values are tested and you feel conflicted. This internal conflict serves as a powerful reminder that something isn't quite right. For instance, imagine you find yourself in a situation where a colleague asks you to cover for them by misleading your boss about a missed deadline. Instantly, you feel a knot in your stomach and a sense of unease. You value honesty and integrity but you feel pressured to go along with it and to be seen as a team player. In the end you give in and go against your values, but the inner discomfort persists. You might tell yourself that it's no big deal to justify your choice, or simply blame your co-worker, but your gut feeling is telling you this decision doesn't sit right.

Not living in alignment with your values can play out in other, more subtle ways too. If you don't value the things that you are doing day in and day out, then it doesn't matter how much money you earn or how many accolades you receive, you'll likely feel as though you're still searching for the 'right' thing. You're likely to feel restless, unsatisfied, direction-less and stuck. You might find yourself working towards the next promotion, a new relationship, another holiday – striving to achieve yet another goal on your list – but that nagging feeling remains. Over and over again you'll keep asking yourself: *What's next?*

We live in an age where pursuing your passion, building your personal brand, forging your own path, and self-expression are paramount, yet many of us struggle to define our sense of self and direction. It's easy to compare ourselves to others and fall into the trap of believing that everyone else has it all figured out. Many people experience moments – or even extended periods – of feeling uncertain, disconnected and purposeless. It is a normal part of life, yet we rarely talk about it openly. Instead, we pretend, and we hide behind a mask of false confidence. We're afraid to admit that we feel lost and stuck for fear of judgement or criticism. But the longer we pretend, the more unsatisfied and stuck we become. I want to reassure you that if you relate to what I am describing here, you are not the only one – and it's never too late to make a change.

If this all feels familiar, trust your instincts. Don't ignore that feeling; it's a warning sign. Remember that red flags serve a purpose. In this instance, your gut is telling you that you're wasting time and energy on things that don't truly matter to you or align with who you are. This is what leads to regrets. We've all heard people say that they regret not spending more time with the people they love, or they regret not travelling and being more adventurous. Some regret spending money *buying* things instead of *doing* things. Perhaps they regret staying in a job or relationship for too long. Deep down, we all recognise the feeling – the one that is difficult to describe – but we often dismiss it. We might be told that we just need to be more resilient, grateful or optimistic. Our first assumption is that *we* are the cause of the problem, and therefore we must change ourselves in order to solve it, instead of considering that perhaps there's a misalignment between our actions and our values. Our surroundings, choices and priorities may need to adjust.

It's easy to overlook how much our environment can impact our well-being. Just as plants need the right conditions to flourish, we can thrive when we are in the right place at the right time and when our needs and values are aligned with those around us. I have more than twenty plants in my house – all different sizes, textures and colours. Over time, my office has become a jungle of lush green leaves. Each plant has its own unique needs, and I've learned how to take care of them through trial and error. Some plants need a lot of water, some need direct sunlight, others prefer shade. A few years ago, I bought two Chinese evergreen plants that looked pretty much the same. I placed one in the hall by the window and one in my bedroom on a corner table. Within a few weeks, these two plants looked completely different. The one in the hall was thriving, soaking up the sun and growing like a leafy supermodel. Meanwhile, the one in my bedroom was looking weak, droopy and depressed. So, in an attempt to revive my sad plant, I moved it to sit alongside the other one in the hall and – ta-da! – within days it was transforming in front of my eyes. No other changes, no special spray or miracle elixir, just a new environment.

When it comes to what we need to grow and thrive, many of us are not all that different from my Chinese evergreens. If we're in a toxic relationship or soul-destroying job, then pretty soon we'll lose our mojo. We'll become unmotivated, fatigued and unhappy, just like the sad plant. Sometimes, instead of trying to reinvent ourselves, we need to recognise that we're in an unsuitable environment. We need to move and find somewhere that we can thrive – whether that means finding more supportive people, a fulfilling job or a community that nourishes us. Thriving tends to happen when our decisions align with our values. Remember, this doesn't always mean flipping your entire life upside down. Even deciding to change one thing can bring you back to your vibrant self.

The mental conflict that occurs when we try to force ourselves to remain in the wrong place or to act in a way that doesn't align with our core values is called 'cognitive dissonance'. You might have experienced it before. It's a confusing feeling, and leads to overthinking and overwhelm. It can feel as though you're following the footsteps of the person who happens to be in front of you, going along with it all for now. If you continue to march on behind them without a compass, you could be walking around in one big circle only to find yourself back where you started. You need to press pause and take a moment to look up and rediscover a sense of direction.

This is where focusing and reminding yourself of your values can really help.

Here's the good news: feeling a lack of direction is not a permanent state; it's a transient phase that we all experience at one point or another. If you choose to embrace this moment of uncertainty, it can serve as a catalyst for growth and transformation. This is not about reinventing yourself, but rediscovering who you already are and then becoming more yourself than ever.

Balancing courage with risk

I've always been impressed by people who are decisive and committed. I can't bear indecision. Anyone can sit on the fence, choose a position of neutrality and refuse to pick a side. I believe we have to be bold in order to make a definitive choice, to speak first, to take action and lead. Decisiveness requires confidence and courage.

Valuing courage is a theme that runs through my life like a red thread. Whether consciously or unconsciously, it impacts every decision that I make. At first, courage might sound like an intangible virtue. Surely everyone values courage? But on closer inspection, I can uncover the reason *why* it is so important to me, and why it ranks so highly in my value hierarchy.

My early years were tough and there's no poetic way around it. I witnessed domestic violence and found myself in situations that required bold action and courage, but as

This is not about reinventing yourself, but rediscovering who you already are and then becoming more yourself than ever.

VALUES

a young girl I felt helpless. If I reflect and consider what my seven-year-old self wanted and needed, it was to have courage and to see my mother summon courage too. Looking back now, I understand that her situation was incredibly difficult and it would be unfair to say that she simply lacked courage. I choose to believe that she did her best. Still, those experiences in my early years sparked something in me. I value courage so highly because I acknowledge it is extremely difficult to uphold without intentional action.

Courage is not about being heroic. I don't run into a burning building without a hose or a plan. That's not courage, that's stupidity. Courage is a willingness to take purposeful action despite initial fear, uncertainty and adversity. But although that might sound good – what does it really mean? Well, here's how valuing courage plays out in my personal and professional decision-making.

Valuing courage means I choose to use my voice. I'm a speaker, an author and a consultant, meaning I get paid to share my ideas. I love the work that I do, but there have been many times when I have felt out of my depth. My fear of criticism and failure seems to grow proportionally to the amount of praise and recognition I receive. Whether I'm delivering a talk to a room full of C-suite executives, recording a podcast interview, writing this book, or giving feedback to a client about a new product, it requires courage to authentically voice my opinions and share my experiences. I once asked a client, 'How candid do you want my feedback to be?' He laughed and said, 'Go for it!'

Valuing courage not only means I can speak with conviction and integrity within my work, it also allows me to enter into difficult conversations and engage in thoughtful disagreements. Whenever possible, I use my voice to advocate for others in an attempt to create an environment where diverse perspectives can be heard. This is not always an easy thing to do, especially as a woman, and especially as a person of colour. But I constantly remind myself that, without courage, we cannot ask questions that challenge prevailing norms and outdated practices, and we will not progress towards something better.

So, when it comes to a seemingly small decision – such as whether to speak up or hold back – I take a deep breath, momentarily pretend that I'm not terrified, take hold of the mic and speak. This isn't something that is always praised or welcomed. I can certainly think of some situations in which I may have been more popular if I'd been more agreeable, but these days I value courage more than I value being liked.

I recognise that it's not always possible for us to live up to our values. You may be wondering what to do in a situation where speaking up has potentially negative consequences. Does making value-led decisions require you to take big risks? I have a somewhat unpopular opinion when it comes to risk-taking and failure. My upbringing and personal experiences mean I do not share the same sentiment as many of today's popular authors, business leaders and podcast hosts. Far too often we're told that our ability to embrace failure and take risks is a prerequisite for success. Tech leaders and billionaires have been telling us for years that their success is in part due to a willingness to fail fast, learn from their mistakes and try again. We are told that risk-taking is aspirational, failure isn't final, and taking risks pays off. But while I understand these ideas and the motivational intention behind them, this advice is far too simplistic. At best, it's ineffective; at worst it's harmful and potentially catastrophic.

In reality, the ability to take risks and recover from failure is a luxury that isn't available to everyone. For some of us, the consequences of failure are not merely setbacks, they could have a devastating impact on financial stability, mental health and even our personal relationships. The narrative that promotes relentless risk-taking tends to gloss over the systemic barriers and inequalities that dictate who gets to fail safely and who doesn't. It's a one-size-fits-all approach that ignores the vast differences in safety nets available to people, which can vary dramatically based on socioeconomic status, family support and professional networks. This culture of celebrating failure often overlooks the emotional toll it takes to keep going and bounce back. Not everyone is wired to see failure as a stepping stone to success. For some, the pressure, stress and shame of failure can lead to anxiety and burnout. We need to have a more nuanced conversation about when and for whom risk-taking is appropriate.

When we read the success stories of the world's elite, we should keep in mind the unique combination of timing, talent, luck, opportunity and privilege that allowed them to take those big risks in the first place. Due to my work as a consultant in wellness technology, I've spent a lot of time with start-up founders and millennial entrepreneurs. Many of them are smart, passionate people trying to create products and services that will improve our health and lives. They have different experiences, interests and skills, and come from different backgrounds, but they typically have one thing in common: their ability to take big risks is amplified by privilege.

Privilege plays a part

'Privilege' is a word that carries a lot of weight, and the mere suggestion that privilege plays a part in our decision-making is often met with resistance, frustration and deep sighs. I want to start off by outlining what privilege is and how it impacts our ability to make decisions, take risks and embrace failure.

Having privilege means that you benefit or have an advantage due to your identity or social group, and it can come in many forms. You can have (or lack) privilege due to gender, race, sexuality, ability, class, age and many other contributing factors. Privilege exists on a scale, and most of it is out of your control. You didn't choose where you were born, the colour of your skin or your sexual orientation. For much of your life, you may not have even noticed your own privilege. We all have privilege in at least one way or another. You don't see it because everybody has it to varying degrees. It's just there – part of the fabric of society. Problems arise when critics mistake its meaning and use it as a blanket term to suggest a person is in some way less deserving of their success. So, let me be clear: privilege does give you an advantage, but it does not mean your entire life has been easy or that you have not worked hard.

When we consider the general consensus about taking risks and embracing failure, we should keep in mind that the path to success is often paved with unspoken advantages. Those who have financial security, influential social networks or access to funds and resources have a much bigger safety net, allowing them to leap and take big risks. While the world champions brave souls who dare to venture out of their comfort zone and 'risk it all', it is crucial to recognise the inherent advantages that make those endeavours possible in the first place. Should a forty-year-old single mother with two children follow the same advice as the twenty-year-old graduate who's living at home with their parents? We are not all in the same position when it comes to taking risks, so we cannot apply the same generic advice and guidance to our unique situations.

Today, I can take risks in some areas of my life because of my current situation and privilege. I have a relative amount of economic security, a supportive network of family and friends, and I've had some good luck along the way. But twenty years ago, it was a different story. When I was sixteen years old, I rented a shared flat in London while studying and working two jobs. At the start of each month, I had to pay rent and bills, I needed enough money to get the train or the bus to work, and any cash that I had was budgeted for food and essentials. One of my jobs was in a shop that paid monthly; the other was a restaurant job that paid in cash at the end of every shift. I figured out that I needed to work an average of twenty-eight hours per week (as well as completing my full-time diploma course, Monday to Friday) to have enough money each month to cover my costs. When there's no safety net, you become hyper-vigilant about seemingly small daily decisions. I remember that whenever I was planning a journey, I would book an off-peak train ticket even if it meant leaving three hours earlier than I needed to. When I finished work at the restaurant, sometimes at 2 a.m., I would walk home instead of spending money on a taxi. Looking back now I can see how dangerous this was. But these are the kinds of decisions I had to make due to necessity.

I've always been ambitious, and I have read countless books about professional athletes, taking inspiration from their work ethic and discipline. I used to watch Tony Robbins talk about visualisation and the power of the mind, and about ten years ago I read *The 4-Hour Workweek* by Tim Ferriss, a book that I can honestly say changed everything for me. But even though I learned a lot from them, I felt as though most of the advice was not applicable to me and my situation at that time. The idea of selling your home and using the money to fund your travel adventures in search of life's meaning is inconceivable when you don't have a home to sell. The majority of the books that I read back then about entrepreneurship and personal development were written by people with very different backgrounds and lifestyles to me. But here's the important part – instead of discarding their ideas and advice because they hadn't been designed for me, I edited and altered them to make them fit.

Perhaps the best thing about growing up with very little is that it makes you more resourceful and inventive with whatever you have. For example, let's say you're shopping and you find a designer suit that's been reduced by 50 per cent, and you try it on but are disappointed to see that it's far too big. What do you do? I'd say, buy the suit and go straight to a tailor. Just because it doesn't fit doesn't mean it's a bad suit. It just needs to be altered and adjusted to make it work for you.

It's exactly the same when it comes to advice: it's not 'one size fits all'. If you've taken generic advice off the shelf and it doesn't fit you, don't be easily discouraged. Instead, remember that you can always examine it further and see if it can be altered in a way that makes it fit. Take it to the tailor. Their job is to transform a pile of fabric into a well-fitting, stylish and useful piece of clothing. This requires technical skills, creativity, attention to detail and practice. We all need to become as skilled as a tailor, and learn how to customise advice.

Some of the ideas that I read in those books were way too big for me back then. I was working weekend shifts at a small restaurant, not running a global company. In order to make them useful, I had to cut them into smaller pieces, be creative and slowly implement the principles in my life over time. Twenty years on, I'm in a very different place, but when I read a book filled with big ideas and thoughtful advice, I still customise it. I consider my own personal goals, my values, and how relevant the advice is to my life right now. This is critical – because the more you understand about yourself and your values, the better you can tailor the advice to fit. Keep this in mind the next time you hear an incredibly wealthy sixty-eight-year-old man (yes, I'm looking at you, Bill) giving out advice. Even if the advice is good, it doesn't mean it's going to be good for you. But don't throw it out – keep it in the back of your wardrobe for a future occasion.

While I'll always be quite cautious when it comes to risk-taking, I have a deep understanding of why I feel this way. A sense of security and assurance ranks highly in my hierarchy of personal values because of my experiences growing up. As a result, over the last ten years I've made decisions that increase my potential future security, such as buying a home and building a pension. I'm not suggesting this is the right thing for everyone to do – values are deeply personal and subjective, and therefore cannot be defined as right or wrong. But once you understand what your values are, and most importantly why you care so much about them, you can begin to make value-led decisions with confidence and ease.

Balancing competing values

Sometimes we find ourselves being pulled in two different directions – torn between two competing values. Picture a situation where a close friend has been working hard on a creative business idea for months and finally asks for your feedback. You really want to be encouraging and supportive, but after hearing their pitch, it's clear to you that the project is flawed and highly unlikely to take off as a viable business. Still, you value kindness, so want to be a supportive friend. Initially, you try to focus on the positive aspects and praise their effort. On the other hand, if you also value honesty, you may feel the urge to give constructive feedback, be real and share your concerns. These two values, while seemingly complementary, are clashing, and you're torn between the desire to be positive and the desire to be honest. In this instance, consider the implications of kindness. It might mean allowing your friend to pursue what appears to be a hopeless dream, potentially wasting time and money. Choosing honesty, however, could lead to hurt feelings and might even risk damaging your friendship. It's a typical dilemma: how do we choose when our key values conflict?

Well, it's possible to strike a balance between the two. By recognising that our values are not mutually exclusive – and that in many cases, both can exist at the same time alongside each other – it's possible to find a harmonious balance between them. You could give truthful feedback that is framed in a constructive way, and emphasise your genuine desire for your friend's success. Sure, they might feel disappointed initially, but in the long run they'll be better off. And you? You'll feel good about your decision, knowing that you stayed true to your value of honesty without compromising on compassion.

Remaining balanced

When faced with choices that pull us in different directions, it's important to remember that life is full of contradictions, inconsistencies and paradoxes. Navigating these complexities requires a thoughtful, nuanced approach – and this cannot be rushed. However, the accelerating pace of modern life rarely allows time for such depth. Often, we feel pressured to make snap judgements in the moment, rather than allowing ourselves time for thoughtful consideration.

When we navigate competing values such as kindness and honesty, we're practising a vital skill – the ability to consider multiple perspectives while remaining balanced. As you scroll through any social media feed you'll see short videos, memes and clickbait content intentionally designed to grab your attention. Most popular social media content is now short-form, so whatever message you're sharing has to be simple, direct and to the point. Research shows that it only takes three seconds for a viewer to decide if they'll continue to watch or scroll past a video in their feed. This is what marketers call 'the three second rule'. They emphasise the importance of capturing a viewer's attention within the first three seconds of any interaction, or else they're gone. This approach means that when we're online, we have a tendency to make snap judgements – to see things as either black or white, for or against, in or out. It can lead to over-simplified debates and a pressure to choose a side, reacting quickly. This same tendency can spill over into our offline lives too, but in reality, most situations are not strictly binary; they are layered with various shades of grey.

The three-second rule takes on a new, almost ruthless efficiency on digital dating platforms like Tinder and Bumble. Users swipe left or right based on a quick glance at someone's photo, often deciding in a few seconds whether a person could be 'the one'. This rapid decision-making process means we might be dismissing a potentially great partner over something as trivial as an awkward smile or a gingham shirt. This habit of making quick judgements can bleed over into other serious decisions, such as sorting through job applications – where candidates can be eliminated based on a split-second scan of their CV.

This demand for speed and efficiency isn't helping us. In fact, when it comes to making decisions, it's tripping us up. We're bypassing the deep, critical thinking necessary for solving complex, nuanced problems, in favour of quick superficial solutions. To counter this trend, we need to make a conscious effort to slow down and engage with the decisions we make in more depth.

Create your own rule book

Understanding your values is one thing, but how can you ensure you're making decisions that are aligned with those values? Creating a set of rules for yourself can be a game changer. Think of these rules as decision hacks. When you're inundated with low-stakes decisions – such as what to wear, what to eat or whether to hit the snooze button – your rules will provide pre-established answers. By deciding certain things ahead of time, you reduce decision fatigue and free up mental space for more critical choices; you enable yourself to make more decisions that matter. Doing so will also help you to make consistent choices, because rather than making a decision based upon how you feel in the moment, you are relying on predefined rules that you established in a considered and meaningful way. It's like having your own value-based playbook for life.

Rules provide us with a sense of structure and predictability in our lives – a sense of calm amongst the chaos. Having a set of rules can also help to reduce the number of decisions we need to make. This is also known as 'cognitive efficiency'. Put simply, rules serve as mental shortcuts that simplify decision-making, instead of us having to evaluate every situation from scratch. Psychologically, there are several key reasons why we tend to follow rules. Often, they align with our moral and ethical values. We have an innate sense of right and wrong, and following rules resonates with our moral compass. We are inherently social creatures, and adhering to rules also helps to maintain social cohesion and harmony within a group. Following rules signals our willingness to cooperate with and make contributions to others. And some rules exist to keep us safe. Our brains are wired to avoid danger, negative outcomes and pain. Sticking to the rules usually helps us to steer clear of trouble, and this reinforces our inclination to follow them. All of this means that when we create a set of rules based upon our own values, we instinctively want to uphold them.

My advice is to keep your rules simple. They should be easy to remember and integrate into your life. Overly complex rules can lead to confusion and are more likely to be forgotten or ignored, whereas simple rules are straightforward and clear, so you're more likely to stick to them. For example: *I don't drink alcohol at work events*; *I invest 10 per cent of my income in index funds*; *I don't check my phone during meals*; *I call my grandparents every Saturday*; *I only drink coffee before midday.* Simple rules such as these are easier to follow.

One of my rules is to go for a walk every day. It doesn't matter when, or where, or for how long, but it has to happen every day. That way, I do not need to engage in the decision burden of deliberating over whether or not to go for a walk each day. Rain or shine, tired or busy, it's non-negotiable. A daily walk is essential for my mind and body; I know the benefits and the science backs it up. A recent study published in the *European Journal of Preventive Cardiology* analysed data on nearly 227,000 people from seventeen studies. It revealed that walking a minimum of 4,000 steps a day significantly reduces your risk of an early death. Motivation indeed! This daily habit has now become an ingrained behaviour, something I do every day without exception. Being proactive about my health and well-being is something I value highly, so this is a rule that feels easy to adhere to.

Having clear rules can also help you to maintain boundaries with others. For example, if someone tells you they're vegetarian, you respect that they don't eat meat because it's their rule. You don't try to persuade them to break it. Typically, we don't argue with rules, because we understand them to be fixed and non-negotiable. So, when you tell someone 'I don't drink at work events' or 'I don't lend money to friends', they'll accept that rule as a decision you've made. Trust me, it's a game changer for navigating social situations and peer pressure.

Your rules can serve as a shield against the overwhelming amount of incoming requests and demands. Inevitably, there will be times when you're tempted to give in, make an exception and bend your rules just to make someone else happy. When this happens, it's time to pause and think. Why did you make these rules in the first place? Each time you stand firm, you're not just sticking to an arbitrary code, you're reaffirming that your values matter.

One of my rules is to never read emails at the weekend. I created this rule after opening an email on a Saturday afternoon that sent me into a tailspin of work-related stress for the rest of the day. I allowed that one seemingly harmless email to disrupt my weekend plans and hijack my state of mind. Now I make sure I stick to the rule of no emails at the weekend, to maintain a clear boundary between my work and personal life. And in doing so, I've eliminated the need to decide whether each incoming email warrants immediate attention or can wait until Monday. This not only preserves family time, it also prevents me from getting distracted and derailed by work.

This rule, like many others, is a result of learning from past experiences and is an action that embodies my values. In truth, it's not really about emails at all, but rather about a pre-made decision and a commitment to maintaining my well-being. If you're someone who struggles to set work-life boundaries, I highly recommend you adopt a rule like this too. Keep in mind that old habits can be hard to break, so don't be surprised if you slip up occasionally. But when this happens, don't throw your new rule book out the window. Instead, remind yourself of the reasons behind the rule you've set, reset and try again.

Here's the latest addition to my rule book: I do not agree to work projects, podcast interviews or speaking gigs with less than seven days' notice. This means I always have enough time to prepare and to arrange childcare if necessary, and it reduces the amount of stress in my life. The downside is that I sometimes miss out on last-minute opportunities, but the upside, yet again, is that my actions align with my values and I keep my well-being intact. You might be wondering – *What if something comes up at the last minute that is just too good to ignore?* I'll admit that if I received an invitation to interview

Michelle Obama at short notice, I'd make an exception to this rule. There will always be situations that require flexibility. Life is unpredictable, and sometimes you may need to adjust your rules to accommodate unique circumstances. The key is to do so mindfully, with awareness of your reasons and limitations.

If you struggle to say no to people's last-minute requests or find that you're easily swayed by the group, having a list of rules is a great way to practise being more assertive. Plus, these pre-decided rules will act as guardrails, preventing you from making impulsive decisions or giving in to pressure and compromising your values.

Having a set of non-negotiable rules does not mean surrendering to a life that is completely automated and boring; it's about a deliberate strategy and intentional living. Ultimately, when you establish – and most importantly stick to – your own rules, you can stop wasting time frequently deliberating over the same choices and start living life on your own terms, one decision at a time.

Creating a personal mission statement

If you've ever worked at a big company, start-up or mission-led organisation, then you'll be familiar with mission statements and company values. The purpose of a mission statement is to ensure that everyone who is working for a company understands the reason that the company exists, the problem they are trying to solve, and why they, as individuals, should show up to work each day. For example, Google's current mission statement is 'to organise the world's information and make it universally accessible and useful', and Disney's mission statement is 'to entertain, inform and inspire people around the globe through the power of unparalleled storytelling'. Tesla's current goal is 'to accelerate the world's transition to sustainable energy'.

For a mission statement to be effective, it must be bold, simple and unambiguous. It should be able to help steer the team in the right direction when making decisions. It can also help them to eliminate distractions and stay focused on the outcome they're trying to achieve. This is why I advise that everyone create their own personal mission statement. This isn't about simply creating a motto or coming up with an inspiring quote for a Pinterest board – it doesn't need to sound impressive or virtuous. The most important thing is that it's authentic and true, so that it gives meaning and purpose to the decisions that you make.

My personal mission statement is 'to encourage ordinary people to achieve extraordinary things'. Whether I'm writing this book, recording a podcast or mentoring a group of young people, my mission remains the same. When I'm presented with a new opportunity, I can quickly tell – often within minutes – if it's going to enable me to deliver on my mission. The pursuit of this mission makes my decisions meaningful.

Having a clear mission statement also helps others to understand who you are, not just what you do. When someone asks me what I do, it can be a little bit awkward. If I give them a vague answer, such as 'I'm a digital entrepreneur', then I'm met with a mixture of confusion and scepticism. I could say that I'm a writer, keynote speaker, broadcaster, content creator, podcast host, coach, strategic advisor and investor. Then I'm pretty sure they'd think I was, in fact, a professional liar. Of course, if I'm asked this question at a social event by a complete stranger then it doesn't really matter what they think – but if you're negotiating a salary or pitching an idea to a book publisher, then it's important for people to understand who you are, what you do and why you do it.

Creating a personal mission statement and identifying your values is not just a one-time activity, it's an ongoing process that takes time and effort. Keep revisiting and refining your values as you encounter new experiences and challenges. If you continually place your values at the centre of your decisions, you'll remain true to yourself and prioritise what matters most.

We've covered a lot in this chapter – from uncovering the roots of where our values come from and how they influence decision-making, to the nuances of balancing competing priorities and maintaining boundaries. Now, armed with this knowledge, it's time to take action and apply this in practical ways. The next time you're facing a high-stakes decision, reflect on your values, your predefined rules and your personal mission statement. Truly knowing your values is an essential step towards clarity and confidence when navigating the complexities of decision-making and modern life.

3

JOY

The science of joy, confronting negativity bias

When was the last time you stopped and questioned which objects, places, experiences and people bring you joy? How often do you visit those places? How often do you see those people? What is your most joyful memory, and who is the most joyful person you know?

Joy, as I understand it, is a state of being that extends beyond momentary positive feeling. It's a deeper, more enduring sense of contentment that enriches our experiences and improves our overall sense of well-being. A life without joy is like living in black and white. Like a bird with no song, or cooking without salt. Sure, you can survive, but where's the flavour? Joy adds that extra dimension – it's the bass guitar, the sauce and sprinkles, an essential ingredient that enhances our lives.

Now, take a step back. If I asked you to consider all aspects of your life, how does joy fit in? Is it something you prioritise, or is it pushed to the bottom of the list due to seemingly more urgent or essential demands? When making important decisions, does joy factor into your choices? Perhaps you believe that joy is limited to a handful of special days and rare moments. Reserved for a week-long holiday drinking wine in

Italy, dancing at a festival in a field full of sequined strangers, or watching your child blow out the candles on their birthday cake. Often, we count down the days as we look forward to these moments. We capture them in a snapshot and they become a framed memory. But while these moments are precious and wonderful, throughout our busy day-to-day lives, joy often finds itself relegated to the periphery.

This is understandable, due to the pressures of modern life; we're often led to believe that every moment not spent working or doing something 'useful' is a wasted opportunity. We feel guilty for indulging in simple pleasures like lounging in the garden with a book or taking a relaxing walk through the park, because there's a nagging voice at the back of our minds telling us that we should be doing something 'better' and 'more valuable' instead. Additionally, as we observe the pace of life accelerating around us, there's a pervasive fear of falling behind. This only amplifies the idea that hobbies and time spent having fun are only permissible if they're contributing to our self-improvement in some way.

But what if we challenge this notion? What if we decided that, instead of allowing joy to lurk in the background of our busy lives, we would intentionally make more space for the things we enjoy? Making the decision to pursue things simply for the sake of enjoyment is not a waste of time; it's a necessary component of a balanced life. If we reframe joy as something important, rather than treating it as an afterthought, then we will no longer feel the need to justify every 'unproductive' moment of our lives.

Finding joy in the everyday

What if I told you that joy does not have to be exceptional and rare? What if I said it's right here, right now, just waiting for you to embrace it? The key to having a more joyful life is much simpler than you think. It's not about waiting for the stars to align, or for the day when everything goes to plan. Joy doesn't need your life to be perfect – it exists amidst the chaos and the imperfections of life too.

Joy can manifest in countless ways. We can find it by connecting with others, spending time with loved ones and creating lasting memories. Choosing acts of creative expression such as painting, singing and writing are all ways of sharing a passion that can elicit feelings of joy. Even the simple act of intentionally noticing moments of beauty in the natural world by watching a sunset, hiking or listening to the sound of the ocean can fill us with a profound sense of joy. I find joy in a bowl of spaghetti topped with fresh basil. In laughing with a friend, singing in the shower, and getting into a bed made with freshly washed sheets. These everyday moments can easily go unnoticed, but when they are savoured and appreciated, they can make us smile and feel gratitude towards our life.

In other words, a more joyful life can be ours the moment we shift our perspective from one of lack to one of abundance, from unappreciative to grateful and from absent to present. When we open our eyes and pay closer attention to

Joy doesn't need your life to be perfect – it exists amidst the chaos and the imperfections of life too.

life's understated and mundane moments, we will realise how charmed life really is. The ordinary can become extraordinary. Now, don't get me wrong, I'm not suggesting that a bowl of spaghetti is going to solve all of life's problems, but it's not a bad place to start!

I'd like you to consider the significance of joy when contemplating decisions that matter. Conventional wisdom might lead us to believe that decision-making requires a cool head and an ability to be unemotional. In some cases, we can rely on data and make a list of pros and cons. However, not all choices can be made this way. Life is not a logical maths problem to solve, and most important decisions aren't measurable in a spreadsheet. When making a high-stakes decision such as committing to a life partner or embarking on a new career, happiness and enjoyment are critical factors that certainly *should* influence the choices we make. Embracing joy doesn't make us naive or idealistic, it makes us human.

When we actively prioritise happiness and joy, it feels like a weight being lifted from the decision-making process. We start to choose people and places that align with our values, confront people-pleasing tendencies, and stop agreeing to things we don't even like. Prioritising joy means confidently saying no based on our own predefined rules and freeing ourselves from overthinking. Trust me, the benefits of prioritising joy can be transformative.

But what's the difference between choosing joy and making emotion-led decisions? Well, one is thoughtful and deliberate, while the other is impulsive and spontaneous. Choosing joy means making a conscious effort to align your decisions with long-term fulfilment and personal values. In contrast, emotion-led decisions are often knee-jerk reactions driven by short-term feelings. Typically, when we react impulsively to an emotion, we're not thinking about the bigger picture, future impact or consequences. On the other hand, choosing joy involves thinking about how our decisions will impact our overall well-being and happiness in the long run.

Joy improves our health

As it relates to overall well-being, the importance of joy cannot be overstated. In fact, research into the relationship between happiness, joy and health is developing quickly and we're still learning about the connection. I've included references to recent, comprehensive studies and journals that explore this topic in depth in the Notes section at the end of the book. It's commonly understood that stress, worry and trauma all have a significant negative impact on physical and mental health. People who have lived in challenging environments and those who have experienced mental or physical abuse are statistically more likely to have poor health outcomes and, in some cases, reduced life expectancy. A lack of joy and happiness is detrimental to our well-being. Experiencing joy, fun and happiness not only makes us feel good, it can actually improve our health.

The American Heart Association has found that 'happiness

leads to healthier behaviours, it helps stave off high blood pressure and excess body fat, resulting in lower risk of stroke and cardiovascular disease'. Experiencing joy and happiness can improve our immune system, relieve stress and pain, and even increase our chances of living longer. In 2017, a meta-analysis looked at sixty-two different studies involving more than 1.25 million people. It found that happiness may actually be a protective force in relation to all-cause mortality.

The science of joy

Joy is not just a momentary state of mind, or a feeling, it is a biological experience that changes our neurochemistry. Let's get into the science. When we experience joy, it triggers specific areas in the brain linked to the reward system and positive feelings. This involves neurotransmitters such as dopamine and serotonin, which are crucial for enhancing our mood. These neurotransmitters, often referred to as 'feel good' chemicals, are released in the brain during enjoyable activities such as eating chocolate, unwrapping gifts, dancing and having sex. They generate pleasure and motivate us to seek similar experiences again and again. This explains why it's hard to resist eating your favourite foods even though you feel full.

Dopamine has a powerful effect, and it elicits positive uplifting emotions, especially when the experience is shared with others. However, this same mechanism can have a downside. In some scenarios, it can lead to compulsive behaviours as we try to recreate that initial rush of feeling good. If unchecked, we can become addicted to things that make us feel good – sugar, alcohol, sex, gambling, shopping, or anything that provides a quick burst of euphoria. However, it's also possible to raise our dopamine levels in a variety of healthier ways; it's all in the decisions we make. For instance, engaging in regular exercise and creative hobbies, spending time with loved ones and practising mindfulness are all ways to elevate our dopamine levels in a positive way.

If you're trying to experience more everyday joy, then exercise-induced dopamine is a great place to start. Exercise not only provides an immediate rise in dopamine levels, it also contributes to long-term regulation. Regular physical activity boosts dopamine activity even during rest, enhancing the brain's reward system over time. Integrating more movement into your daily routine – like choosing to cycle to work rather than take the bus – can raise dopamine levels and enhance joy. This is another example of low-impact decisions creating a significant change to the quality of your life when repeated day after day.

The *UK Fitness Report* is an annual deep dive into the nation's attitude to health. The 2023–24 edition found that modern working life has a clear impact: 41 per cent of people said they were simply too tired after work to exercise, while 34 per cent stated their job didn't leave them enough time to exercise. The report also found that the benefits of physical activity were clear to see – 36 per cent of people that exercised said that they had seen an improvement in their mental health, mood, anxiety and stress levels, as well as fewer feelings of depression.

The report shows a clear trend: even though we know regular exercise makes us feel good, so many of us are still not able to prioritise it. It's easy to get caught up in the perpetual motion of being 'too busy'. The demands of work, family and personal commitments can take up every hour of every day if we let them. But living in a constant state of busyness comes at a cost. It can cause us to neglect our relationships, forgo self-care and ultimately defer our own happiness. If we do not prioritise joy and happiness today, we risk delaying it until tomorrow, next week, next year, and so on. Are you too busy to exercise? Too busy to rest? Too busy to spend time with friends? When did you become too busy for joy? Life is too damn short to be too busy for joy, my friend. It's not about abandoning responsibilities, but about redefining them and making choices that consider all aspects of well-being. We have to rebel against busyness and reclaim our right to experience joy!

Highs and lows

Ever notice how some people tend to see the downside in every situation? It can seem as though negativity is their default setting. When you ask about their recent holiday to the Caribbean, they tell you that the weather was unbearably hot, the resort was too busy and the mosquito bites ruined the whole trip. When you congratulate them on their job promotion, they let out an exasperated sigh and tell you how the new role requires longer hours, more meetings and a terrible boss. They tend to go through life with a glass-half-empty attitude. Then there are other people who seem naturally inclined to look on the bright side and have a more optimistic approach to life. When they're stuck in traffic, they use the extra time to catch up on their favourite podcast or enjoy listening to the radio. If they're facing a challenging work project, they see it as an opportunity to learn and gain experience on the job.

Well, there's an explanation for this difference.

In an interview with Tim Ferriss, Dr Arthur Brooks – a professor at Harvard Business School known for his popular course on happiness – mentions how 'there's a big mistake that almost everybody makes about happiness, which is they believe that happiness is the absence of unhappiness. That's wrong, happiness and unhappiness are not opposites and the two can co-exist.' At Harvard, Dr Brooks shares a test with his students called the Positive and Negative Affect Schedule (PANAS). This refers to the emotions or feelings that you might experience, and how both influence you to act and make decisions. 'Positive affectivity' refers to positive emotions and expressions such as joy, cheerfulness and contentment. 'Negative affectivity', on the other hand, refers to negative emotions and expressions such as anger, fear and sadness.

The test is pretty simple: it consists of twenty words that describe different emotions, such as 'guilty', 'determined', 'ashamed', 'proud', etc. Participants are instructed to score each of the emotions on a scale of one to five, to correspond with how they generally feel about life.

Dr Brooks has designed four profiles to help us understand the results of this test: Cheerleader, Mad Scientist, Poet and Judge.

- If you tend to express a lot of positive affectivity, and little negative affect, you are a Cheerleader. You have lots of good moods and not too many bad moods.
- If you are high for both positive and negative, you are a Mad Scientist. You have lots of strong emotions, both good and bad.
- If you tend to show high negative affectivity and low positive affectivity, you are a Poet. Lots of bad moods, fewer good moods.
- If you are low on both, you are a Judge. You don't have lots of strong emotions on either side. You're really steady.

Dr Brooks stresses that none of these profiles is either good or bad, they're simply an indication of your most natural disposition. Even the most optimistic people experience disappointments and frustrations, just like anyone else. What sets them apart is their perspective.

By choosing to focus on solutions rather than problems, and by embracing curiosity and optimism, you can cultivate a mindset that leads to a more fulfilling and happier life. This doesn't mean ignoring problems or negative emotions. You can choose to focus on the positive aspects of your life while also acknowledging the negatives; both can co-exist. But by becoming aware of your default mode, you can make conscious choices to manage and influence your emotions and approach decision-making with a more balanced outlook.

Sharing joy with others

Did you know that it is possible to experience vicarious joy? This happens when we see someone that we love and care about experiencing good fortune, achieving their goals and finding their slice of happiness. By celebrating their achievements, we get to share those positive feelings with them, and our own lives get a little brighter too. That's why I love going to weddings. I listen to every word that is said during the ceremony and I feel an excitable energy in the pit of my stomach. It's one of the most special and beautiful moments of a person's life, and I truly enjoy witnessing and celebrating the intense emotions of their love and happiness.

Experiencing joy through others is a wonderful way to cultivate a happier life. Practise celebrating your friend's promotion, become a cheerleader when your kids score a goal, and encourage those around you to share their good news stories. Ask your friends what they are looking forward to next summer, if they've read any good books recently; even better, ask them about their dreams and aspirations. It will be a much more enjoyable conversation than the tired old rant about the weather, or gossiping about someone else.

And on that same point, beware of schadenfreude. This German word describes the odd experience of pleasure, joy or satisfaction that comes from learning of or witnessing the failure or humiliation of someone else. I once worked with someone who seemed to enjoy delivering bad news. He would try his best to conceal it, but his gleaming eyes and smirk always gave it away. It was obvious to me that he was secretly pleased to be the messenger of bad news, like a mean kid who wanted to ruin everyone's day. Steer clear of these people as much as you can. If that's not possible, remember that you have the tools to make decisions that honour your values, priorities and emotional boundaries. This kind of behaviour says more about them than it does about anyone else. Often, people who delight in the misfortunes of others are doing so to mitigate their own feelings of unhappiness and dissatisfaction.

The next time someone's dishing out good news, pay attention to your reaction. Do you share their feelings of joy? Do you notice a twinge of rivalry – as if, somehow, by them winning, it means you're losing? Do you congratulate them publicly but later commiserate with yourself alone? It's natural to feel envy from time to time. It's an unavoidable human emotion, so don't beat yourself up about it. But notice the emotion you're feeling and use it as feedback. Envy can highlight things that you want or would like to pursue yourself. When you feel a pang of this emotion – perhaps because someone has achieved or accomplished something that you also desire – rather than letting it consume you or trying to resist it, take it as a signal directing you towards your own aspirations. Ask yourself what exactly it is that you are envious of. Is it their new job, their adventurous travels, or perhaps something less tangible such as their confidence? These feelings can help you to set your own goals and provide you with a clearer sense of direction. Envy can help you to discover what's missing in your life; let it inspire you to pursue happiness intentionally, without diminishing your ability to share in others' joy.

An effective tool for understanding our emotions is to journal about them. 'Meta-emotion' refers to the feelings we have about our feelings. For instance, we might feel guilty about feeling envious, or proud of ourselves for feeling happy about someone else's success. The ability to recognise and accept meta-emotions helps us to become more self-aware and self-compassionate. And it can turn a feeling such as envy from a negative emotion into a motivating force. Start off by noting down what happened to trigger the emotion, reflect on what it reveals about your own desires, and set some goals to achieve something similar in your own life.

Understanding our emotions not only benefits our personal growth, it also influences the way we interact with others. It's possible to create joy and spread positive emotions both intentionally and unintentionally via our actions, behaviour and body language. 'Emotional contagion' is a fascinating phenomenon in which emotions can be transferred from one person to another. It's a powerful form of social influence that operates effortlessly within our interactions – small gestures such as holding the door for a stranger, waving to your neighbour and giving up your seat for someone else can start a Mexican wave of positive energy. If you want to see joyful emotional contagion in full effect, go to YouTube right now and search for 'Jon Bon Jovi Park Singing by a Guy'. It's impossible to watch that video without smiling and eventually singing along too. But even if you're not a great singer, try to find a way to spread a bit of joy to those around you today. And seriously, go watch that video before you read any further!

Why is pursuing joy so hard?

It's understandable to question how joy can fit in with the many challenges we face in the modern world. There are moments when we might feel as though seeking joy isn't worthwhile. We can become weighed down by the negativity around us. In the past, I felt frustrated when I met people who seemed nonchalant and unenthusiastic. I'd think, *Don't take yourself seriously. Why not let yourself be excited and have some fun?* My instinct was to encourage them to embrace joy. However, doing research for this book has prompted a shift in my perspective. What I've come to realise is that, for some, a lack of enthusiasm and a reluctance to embrace joy stems from past struggles and disappointments – or it could be that they're just wired that way. Sometimes (re)discovering joy needs patience and a more compassionate approach.

In a way, it's easy to understand why some people struggle to embrace this vital emotion. In recent years, we've been living through a global pandemic, a cost-of-living crisis and countries at war. We've unleashed new AI technologies with the potential to disrupt every industry. Global economic instability and the climate crisis have become the norm. It's no wonder we're stressed out. When you wake up and turn on the radio or glance at your phone, you're likely to hear or see headlines about war, mass shootings, global warming and pending devastation. It's natural to feel a sense of unease. And as this continues daily, then over time, our fear, anxiety and stress intensify.

Let's face it, these challenges are all real and worthy of our attention, but we cannot surrender to overwhelm and despair. We must not be convinced that there is nothing left to be joyful about. Amidst the chaos, finding moments of joy is more important than ever for maintaining our sanity and resilience. When everything around us seems fixated on selling discontentment, choosing to find joy in the small moments feels like an act of rebellion. And sure, this is not an easy thing to do, in part because it requires us to go against our natural instincts and our brain's evolutionary inclination towards negativity and scanning potential dangers. This is due to a powerful force known as 'negative brain bias' – the brain's tendency to pay more attention to negative information than to positive.

This bias was discovered and documented by psychologists Paul Rozin and Edward Royzman, who showed that across almost all domains of life, we generally give more importance to negative experiences than to positive or neutral experiences. In turn, the bias influences the language we use to describe our emotions. Research conducted at Penn State noted that 'people know more negative emotion words than positive or neutral words. The proportion of words was 50 percent negative, 30 percent positive and 20 percent neutral.'

Even our memories can be influenced by the negativity bias. This form of selective attention means that we tend to pay more attention to negative memories, as we are more likely to perceive them as relevant and important. If you've ever been in an accident or witnessed one, you can probably still remember it in detail, even years later. Negative events require more cognitive processing, and so retain a stronger presence in our memories. In contrast, positive experiences do not trigger the same level of cognitive response or attention, making them more likely to be downplayed or forgotten over time.

This cognitive selectivity is rooted in our evolutionary history. Negative brain bias is essentially a survival mechanism designed to keep us safe from potential threats and dangers. Evolving to pay more attention to negative stimuli provided an advantage for our ancestors when they needed to stay vigilant to avoid harm in dangerous environments. The sound of a cheetah in the bushes was something they needed to pay attention to because failing to do so was a matter of life and death. And even in today's relatively safer world, we are still primed to pay attention to danger – so our brains retain this bias.

In addition, we now live in a world where we have to contend with modern media dynamics. In a digital-first world, information travels quickly. News channels and social media entities are businesses with profit-driven incentives. Sensational and negative news stories tend to shock and captivate audiences in a way that feel-good news stories don't. Sadly, negative news tends to generate more reactions, likes, shares, comments and clicks than positive ones. After all, a heartwarming act of kindness might make us smile, but disasters or conflicts draw our attention like a magnet. As I mentioned previously, the content we see on our social media feeds is designed to grab our attention, maximise engagement and keep us coming back for more. The online algorithms learn from our behaviours and tailor our social media feeds to show similar content. This perpetuates a cycle that leads to an endless supply of negative content.

But let's return to the idea that our brains are hardwired to notice danger. Although once beneficial, in today's context this bias can distort our perception of reality, hindering rational decision-making. Picture this: you're considering moving house from a busy city to a much greener area. At first, you're optimistic about the idea and you even start to picture yourself waking up on a Saturday morning to walk your dog through a beautiful park. You're pretty sure that moving to the countryside means you'll be able to buy a bigger place, you'll enjoy better air quality and less noise pollution, plus you'll be able to save some cash by reducing your overall living expenses. It all feels good until the negative brain bias slaps you in the face, waking you up from this idyllic daydream.

Before long, you'll find that these positive thoughts about moving are replaced with ideas for all the things that could go wrong. You find yourself wondering if you really want the stress of uprooting your life, thinking that you'll miss that great deli in your neighbourhood, dreading your weekly commute, and worrying about your future neighbours. And on and on. You may even recall a story you heard on a true crime podcast about a person who left the city in pursuit of the good life. Despite the fact you never made it to the end of that particular episode, given the title of the podcast series, you can probably guess how it ended for them! Your brain quickly becomes hyper-focused on all the potential negatives and starts to create an unbalanced perspective, hindering your ability to make a rational decision. Negative brain bias causes you to focus excessively on the potential downsides, magnifying minor inconveniences – such as a forty-minute commute – so they become obstacles, catastrophes and reasons to avoid change. After just a few minutes of listing all of the things that could potentially go wrong and lead to disaster, your concerns and fears overshadow your initial excitement and you decide to forget all about it. Pessimism beats optimism, 1–0.

If we allow the powerful influence of our brain's negativity bias to go unchecked and unchallenged, it will cloud our judgement and potentially hold us back from pursuing our passions and making decisions that will lead to an enriching and joyful life. This is why it's important to counteract our brain's factory settings, override the default software and overcome the bias. We can do this by consciously redirecting our attention towards more positive aspects and possibilities. This doesn't mean ignoring all risks or being oblivious to potential downsides, but instead balancing our thinking by actively considering the positive outcomes and opportunities that might lie ahead.

By consciously training our minds to recognise the positives, we can challenge the instinctive negativity bias and make decisions based on a much more balanced perspective. The act of consciously counteracting this bias takes time, practice and patience. Here's a simple way to approach it. Imagine your mind is like a spotlight on a stage. When you notice something negative, it's as if the spotlight gets directed solely onto that one negative thought, highlighting it and making everything else fade into the background. Positive thoughts and events will naturally get a lot less attention unless we actively decide to shine the spotlight on them. So, if you want to make fair and balanced decisions, make sure you're giving equal attention to both sides of the stage. Remember that you can train your brain to look for the upside, remember the wins, and make more decisions in the name of happiness and joy. All training requires us to put in the time, effort and energy, so why not start right now? Here are three things you can do each day to counteract the negativity bias . . .

1. Practise using optimistic language

Pay attention to the words you use in conversation, both with others and with yourself. Try to avoid saying words that are self-deprecating and self-critical. Negative self-talk can be incredibly detrimental to your mental well-being and overall confidence. When we constantly criticise or speak negatively about ourselves, we reinforce a cycle of low self-esteem and self-doubt. A habit that not only diminishes our perception of ourselves, but can even impact how others perceive us. In British culture, self-deprecation is often seen as a form of modesty or humility. It's quite common to downplay our own achievements and talents, perhaps as a way to avoid appearing arrogant or boastful. This tendency towards self-deprecation is often learned at a young age. At school, I remember being called a 'show off' after winning an award in front of my classmates. It's ironic really – we're encouraged to achieve (we'll discuss this in more detail in Chapter 4) but then we're so often criticised when we do.

Irrespective of the reason, constantly belittling ourselves can have real consequences. When we talk negatively and undervalue ourselves in front of others, it can lead them to doubt us and our capabilities. People may even perceive us as lacking confidence and begin to question whether we are indeed competent enough. Would you choose a team captain who didn't believe they could win?

To combat this tendency towards negative self-talk, it's important to practise using optimistic language both in your internal dialogue and your conversations with others. Instead of focusing on your faults, acknowledge your strengths and abilities. By reframing your thoughts and words in a more positive way, you can improve your sense of self-esteem and overcome the negativity bias that fuels self-doubt.

2. Seek uplifting content

Counterbalance the negativity bias by actively seeking out positive and uplifting content. Deliberately looking for sources of optimism and positivity can offset the pervasive negativity in today's media landscape. One way to do this is by immersing yourself in literature. That might be fantasy and adventure books – anything that allows you to engage your imagination and momentarily escape reality. Another way is to follow social media accounts that fill your feed with laughter and joy, whether it's fun memes, uplifting stories, cute pet videos, or anything else that simply brightens your day. You could also make it a part of your daily routine to listen to uplifting music. While music is subjective and what we each like is different, the undeniable truth is that it has a universal power to influence our mood and mindset. Lastly, for a guaranteed mood boost, comedy podcasts can provide you with a daily dose of laughter medicine and offer a break from modern-day stressors.

JOY

Here are some of my favourites . . .

READ

The Alchemist by Paulo Coelho
The Secret Life of Bees by Sue Monk Kidd

WATCH

Up – a film by Disney Pixar
Some Like It Hot – an old classic starring Marilyn Monroe
The Greatest Night in Pop – a documentary on Netflix

LISTEN

Songs in the Key of Life – Stevie Wonder
Greatest Hits – Queen
Motown Anthems

DOWNLOAD

The Laughs of Your Life podcast, with Doireann Garrihy
Closet Confessions podcast, with Candice Brathwaite and Coco Sarel

Taking time to seek out uplifting content can help to balance out our tendency to focus on the negative, giving us a more rounded view of life. When we immerse ourselves in uplifting stories, music and media, it reminds us of the good things in life. Making this a part of our routine can boost our mood and support overall well-being.

3. Limit negative news consumption

When it comes to staying informed about what's happening in the world, it's essential to strike a balance between being aware and becoming overwhelmed. One effective strategy is to limit your consumption of negative news. Instead of immersing yourself in a constant stream of doom and gloom, consider adopting a more mindful approach to news consumption. A practical tip is to read news headlines and stories for no more than fifteen minutes each day. This allows you to stay informed about major events without feeling as though you're drowning in a sea of negativity. Be selective about the sources you rely on for news – choose reputable sources that offer a somewhat balanced view of the world, rather than sensationalising the headlines for likes or clicks. Lastly, don't look at social media first thing in the morning or last thing at night, as this can set a negative tone for your day or interfere with your ability to unwind and relax before you fall asleep.

By practising these simple strategies, you can cultivate

a healthy relationship with news media and stay informed while also preserving your mental and emotional well-being. This allows you to maintain a more balanced perspective of the world, without constant alerts inspiring outrage and negativity.

Years ago, when I worked in fitness studios, I was often required to complete risk assessment forms. As someone with an allergy to admin, this was my least favourite part of the job. It's a simple five-step process: Identify hazards. Decide who might be at risk and how. Evaluate the risks and implement precautions. Record your findings. Review your assessment and update when necessary. (Are you yawning yet?) This is similar to what's going on in your brain when you're trying to make a decision. It's walking around wearing a fluorescent hard hat, carrying a clipboard and looking out for risks and danger. Your brain is ready to present you with a thorough risk assessment in any situation, because it was not designed to make you happy, it was designed to keep you safe. So remember that, the next time your brain asks: *What could go wrong? What if I'm making a mistake? How can I be certain this is going to work out? What if I don't enjoy it?* To counteract it, ask these questions in response: *What could go right? What's the best possible scenario? What if it turns out better than I could have ever imagined?* And if you're still competing with the negative brain bias, try the following exercise:

> **CONFRONTING NEGATIVITY BIAS**
>
> Think about a decision you're currently facing and start to imagine the worst-case scenario. Don't freak out, bear with me, there's a valid reason for this. By confronting the worst potential outcome, you can start to explore ways to cope and move forward, even when things might not go to plan.
>
> Next, grab a blank sheet of paper and a pen, take a deep breath and answer the following two questions:
>
> 1. What is the worst thing that could happen?
> 2. If the worst thing does happen, what will I do next?

I've used this exercise many times when fear is flooding my brain and overwhelming my thoughts with doomsday scenarios. In my experience, whenever I answer the first question – 'What's the worst thing that can happen?' – I realise that, however terrifying the answer is, it always helps to answer the second question. If the worst thing does happen, what will I do next? This reminds me that, whatever happens, it will not be the end of my life. Asking myself what I will do next means that life will go on, and it gives me a sense of empowerment because I still get to make a choice. We cannot control everything that happens in life, but we can control how we respond to events. This exercise is a way to acknowledge our fears and concerns without letting them hold us back.

How can you let go of guilt?

When we were young, we took every opportunity to enjoy ourselves. Why walk to school, when we could run, jump, and climb over walls and tree stumps along the way? Many of us experienced joy by riding our bikes, playing board games, drawing pictures, building Lego houses and creating stories. But at some point, playtime was over, and it was time to focus and do something more productive with our time. A few years later, our days consist of meetings, replying to emails, rescheduling dental appointments and endless laundry – also known as 'adulting'. Yes, we've even added this word to the dictionary. It describes behaviour that is seen as responsible and grown-up, such as paying bills and running errands.

So, adulting begins and our schedules get filled. We're convinced that busyness is normal because everyone around us is busy too. This is compounded further by the fact that we live in a world that is obsessed with achievement, progress and growth. We've been led to believe that joy is something that should be earned, reserved for the weekend, postponed until everything else is done. Joy is viewed by our modern culture as a luxury, and our perception that joy is a rare indulgence stems from a misunderstanding of its true meaning and importance.

Let's pause for a moment to focus on the word 'luxury'. The word itself conjures up images of extravagance and indulgence. But what does 'luxury' mean to you? For me, life's luxurious moments can be as simple as enjoying breakfast in the garden. As I take the first sip of my coffee, close my eyes and turn my face towards the warmth of the sun, it's a moment of joy that I savour, and it feels luxurious to indulge in it. What small thing could you do this week to create a moment of luxury? You don't have to justify it, no need to earn it, you can simply choose to enjoy it.

Luxury is typically associated with money, but for many of us, the momentary joy of spending money is entangled with hesitation and feelings of guilt. We each have a unique relationship with money and how we choose to spend it. This relationship is a combination of personal belief, past experiences and societal norms. But it's important to unravel this web and take a moment for introspection.

Many of us have been conditioned to equate spending with frivolity, so we feel guilty for spending money on things that are non-essential. Our ideas about money can be traced back to a variety of factors. For example, if we were raised in a home where frugality and saving were emphasised, then we might have carried those attitudes into adulthood. As a result, we could find it difficult to enjoy spending money even when we can afford it. Financial hardship and scarcity may have had a lasting impact on our spending habits, and we might feel the need to diligently save money due to a fear of it running out.

Even if you're not harbouring any deep emotional

issues related to money, it's likely that your ability to enjoy spending money could still be impacted by other factors such as uncertainty about the future, job insecurity, economic instability, or simply wanting to avoid consumerism and wastefulness. Do you really need another pair of jeans? We're constantly battling with conflicting emotions and barriers that make it difficult to genuinely enjoy spending money, even when we've worked hard to get it. How would you experience the joy of spending money without feeling burdened by guilt? I'm not talking about reckless spending, but about giving yourself permission to enjoy spending money on experiences that have the potential to enrich your life – and buying things that bring genuine feelings of joy.

Consider this hypothetical scenario: I'm handing you an envelope that contains £500 in cash; the money is a gift but there are two conditions. One: you must spend the money on something that brings you joy. Two: you must spend the money within twenty-four hours. What would you do with it? Maybe you'd buy a new pair of boots, or invite some friends to join you for dinner and cocktails at your favourite restaurant. Maybe you'd invest the money in the stock market or donate the money to charity, or maybe you'd spend it on a return ticket from London to Paris. Whatever you choose to do with the cash is up to you, but most importantly, you have to enjoy spending it guilt-free.

Now imagine doing the exact same thing again, this time

with £100, and then try it with just £10. Get creative, and you might be surprised by what you can do with just £10 or even less. Last year I bought three books from a charity shop for £5. My stepdaughter read the entire trilogy from start to finish and those books brought her hours of joy.

It's interesting and fun to notice which things come immediately to mind when you think about how you're going to spend the money. While writing this, I was intrigued to see how some of my friends would respond to this question, so I sent it to them via email. Within minutes, I received responses ranging from 'I'd sign up to a course' to 'Obviously I'd spend it on Botox'. I guess joy really is subjective!

The Joyful Spending Allowance

Balancing the importance of joy and managing financial responsibilities is the reason I created a 'Joyful Spending Allowance' or JSA, and I'm urging you to do the same. It not only provides a framework for joyful, guilt-free spending, but can also reduce stress and overthinking – especially when making low-stakes decisions.

The concept of a JSA revolves around setting aside a portion of your income specifically designated for joyful spending. This could be a percentage of each paycheck or a fixed amount, depending on your financial situation. Whether it's 10 per cent of your earnings or a budget of £300 per month, the rules for creating a Joyful Spending Allowance remain the same. First, ensure that this allocation is financially feasible – in other words, it has to be money that you can afford without incurring debt or using credit. Second, you must grant yourself permission to enjoy the experiences or purchases that bring you genuine happiness, free from the burden of guilt. Each time you spend the money from your JSA, it's a conscious choice – and a moment of reward for past efforts.

By creating this framework, you're also distinguishing between responsible spending and reckless splurging. Impulsive purchases are often driven by short-lived dopamine highs – we'll explore this more in the next chapter – whereas joyful spending is a more deliberate choice that prioritises long-term satisfaction. A JSA is about mindful decision-making, and when used correctly it can help you to feel more gratitude and less guilt about the things you choose.

Personally, I've realised I enjoy spending money on experiences rather than items, and I'll admit I learned this the hard way. Spending money on dinner with friends has never left me feeling regretful. However, I've occasionally discovered unused gym equipment in the garage that I no longer want and it's clear this was a waste of money. The most expensive things on my JSA list are usually aeroplane tickets and live music events. Travelling, for me, is an unparalleled joy that makes spending money worthwhile in every sense. I've decided that any money I spend travelling is an investment in joy and therefore is money well spent.

Is comparison getting in the way of your joy?

You've probably heard that 'comparison is the thief of joy'. If we let ourselves be consumed by comparisons to those who appear to have much more than us, then we trap ourselves in an endless cycle of dissatisfaction and unhappiness. If we flip the lens and focus on comparing ourselves to those who have much less, we might feel momentary gratitude, but it's likely we'll also feel an inflated sense of superiority as we attribute that to working harder.

Most of us accept that there will always be someone who is seemingly better off. Someone smarter, more attractive, richer, happier or more fortunate than us. We might feel envious of them, and we might even say that we don't like them much – when in fact, deep down, we wish we could be more like them. You see, comparison is a double-edged sword. We each have an inherent desire for self-improvement and progression. It's human nature to compare ourselves and our lives to those around us, and it's natural to aspire to having or achieving more. The problem is that often we haven't defined what 'more' is, and so we continue to chase an ever-receding horizon. The modern world, driven by the relentless pursuit of perfection, has birthed an insidious culture of comparison. When it comes to decision-making, comparison is not only the thief of joy, comparison is the enemy of satisfaction.

The more we succumb to the allure of comparison, the

less likely we are to be happy with our final choice. Comparison clouds our thinking, distorts our judgement and leaves us second-guessing ourselves. If we focus too much on what others are trying to achieve and attain, we inevitably lose sight of what truly matters to us. This lack of clarity is amplified further when we observe the choices of others – a phenomenon known as 'social proofing'. Put simply, social proofing is the influence of seeing others do something, leading us to believe it's a good idea or the correct choice. When we observe other people following a trend, buying a product or supporting an idea, we tend to follow suit and go along with it too, because we assume it must be right. Social proofing sneaks into our subconscious, shaping our choices in subtle ways – often without us realising it – and it can easily lead to conformity and a lack of independent thinking.

The next time you go out for dinner with a group of people, observe how social proofing influences your decision-making. Even relatively small decisions such as whether to order alcohol or how much to tip are likely to be influenced by other people's preferences. This might not seem like a big deal; so what if you go along with the group decision instead of making an independent choice – it's just one dinner after all! But when we look at the influence of social proofing on our habits, actions and behaviours over time, it becomes clear that who we spend time with matters a lot.

If you spend your time with a group that drinks a lot, it's likely you will do the same. If you spend a lot of time with a group that exercises a lot, you will likely do the same. If you spend a lot of time with a group that prioritises joy, it's likely you will do the same. Social proofing isn't necessarily a bad thing, but it's important to be aware of it for a number of reasons. Firstly, it can blind us to alternative perspectives and ideas. A subconscious fear of going against the status quo can discourage us from exploring other possibilities. Secondly, if we consistently ignore our own desires, eventually we don't even know what we really like and want. We may find ourselves making decisions that do not align with who we are, pandering to other people's requests, and more importantly, we may find ourselves making decisions that do not bring lasting and true joy.

So, the next time you're faced with a decision and you suspect that social proofing is hindering your ability to think clearly, try answering these questions:

- If nobody else could see me or was aware of my choice, would I still make this decision?
- Is this the best option for me, or am I choosing what's best for everyone else?
- If I go along with the group consensus, am I likely to regret it?
- Who is most likely to benefit from this decision?

Remind yourself of your personal values, practise independent thinking, and notice when you find yourself being pulled along by the group. Social proofing influences us all to some extent, so surround yourself with diverse perspectives and people who want more for you, not more from you – people who bring you joy.

Embracing joy is not merely a nice-to-have; it's essential for a balanced life. I cannot emphasise this enough. We don't have to wait for a big, once-in-a-lifetime moment to fully embrace joy; we can find it in the simple pleasures, the everyday moments that are often overlooked. By understanding the science behind joy and challenging our brain's negativity bias, we can begin to make balanced decisions that lead to greater happiness. Embracing joy isn't just about making ourselves feel good – we can pass it on to others too. In doing so, we continue to increase our happiness and overall well-being. So, let's rebel against the never-ending cycle of busyness and the demands of the modern world. I'm urging you to start making decisions that prioritise happiness and help you reclaim your right to joy!

4

SUCCESS

Redefining success, seasons of success, the personal ambition paradox

If you search for books about success, you'll find hundreds to choose from. Do you want to build a thriving business? Create meaningful and long-lasting relationships? Raise successful kids? (Yes, there's even a book for that.) What it comes down to is one question: Do you want to learn how to construct a life of purpose, achievement and great reward? Of course you do – we all do. When we read the business strategies of tech giants, the training routines of pro athletes and the mindfulness practices of gurus, we can draw inspiration from the stories of those who have achieved success in the past. We can study their habits, read about their wins and failures, and gain insight into their decision-making processes.

Take Jeff Bezos, founder and former CEO of Amazon, the world's largest online retailer. Bezos talks about the concept of 'type 1' and 'type 2' decisions. In his view, type 1 decisions are irreversible and so must be made carefully. These are closed-door decisions, meaning once you enter, the door closes and locks behind you and there's no going back. On the other hand, type 2 decisions are like revolving doors you can walk through and then walk back out of if necessary. When I first read about Bezos's decision-making concept, it got me thinking about the number of times I had agonised over a decision as though it were an irreversible life-and-death situation, when in fact I could reverse the decision and try again if I needed to. Perhaps it would be inconvenient, but not the end of the world.

The route to success is often painted as a linear path, a direct climb to the top. But ask anyone you admire about their journey, and they'll likely tell you that it was not without many wrong turns, mistakes and hard lessons. They've walked back out of several revolving doors, and sometimes they've even pushed through closed ones. Rarely in life do things remain permanent, and success is never the result of a single pivotal decision, but rather the sum of all the choices made along the way.

How can we define success?

'Success' is a word that has become burdened with layers of meaning and pressure. The idea you've created in your mind of what it means to be successful is likely to be heavily influenced by your culture and lifestyle, as well as your past experiences and future aspirations. Over time, each of us has attached words and images to the idea of what 'success' looks like. Words such as 'wealth', 'confidence', 'fame' and 'talent'. Or maybe 'purpose', 'influence', 'pioneer' and 'visionary'.

What it means to be successful can vary greatly depending on social context, your personal values and your current circumstances.

Naturally, we each have a strong desire to succeed in life, partly because we've been led to believe that the more success we have, the happier we will be. It's a universal idea that is understood by the child in the classroom dreaming of becoming a prize-winning scientist as well as the corporate executive striving for a promotion. The pursuit of success undoubtedly shapes our goals, aspirations and many of our decisions.

In its most basic form, success literally means *to succeed* and to accomplish a goal that you've set out to achieve. Okay, that seems straightforward enough, but it's also too simple a definition for today's complex world. Success is a far more multifaceted and nuanced notion that varies depending on where in the world you live and how others around you think about success, as well as other contributing factors relating to personal values (as discussed in Chapter 2).

A cultural view of success

When it comes to defining success, people who were raised in Western cultures often adopt an individualistic outlook. This perspective places significant emphasis on qualities such as individuality, autonomy, self-reliance and self-sufficiency. Decision-making, in this context, revolves around personal gain and individual achievement. We are encouraged to pursue our own goals and interests; to do whatever it takes, sometimes at the expense of everyone else. Western cultures tend to prioritise speed and efficiency, hence decisions need to be made quickly; it's time-consuming to consider multiple opinions and get approval from all stakeholders. Living in a highly competitive environment can lead us to make decisions that prioritise our personal success over collective gain. In individualistic cultures, we celebrate and praise those described as 'self-made' rather than acknowledging the effort and support of an entire team.

In contrast, in collectivist cultures such as Japan, there is a much greater focus on collaboration and achieving shared goals. Traits like selflessness, loyalty and altruism are highly valued. Imagine a group that is trying to solve a problem and working towards a clearly defined goal. In this scenario, each member's mindset is one of collaboration rather than competition. There's a shift away from *They can't do this without me* towards *I can't do this without them*. People in collectivist cultures view the success and well-being of the group as more important than individual success. There is a sense of shared responsibility and mutual support.

Collectivism can also have its downsides, of course. There can be an emphasis on conformity – adhering to social norms and expectations. Decisions are often made collectively, with input from various members of the group. Deviating from social norms might be met with disapproval, or even sanctions. Building and maintaining harmonious relationships is crucial for social coherence, so people may seek to avoid conflict.

Understanding cultural nuance is crucial for navigating decision-making in the modern world. Just as our values can be inherited from others, being aware of different cultural influences can help us to identify how our own background may be unknowingly influencing our decision-making process.

It's understandable that if we grew up in Western culture, we might inherently believe in the notion of 'winner takes all'. This explains why many of us grew up feeling as though life is an ongoing test to pass. A belief that we must measure, score and even rank ourselves based on our achievements starts at school, with yearly report cards, tests, grades, first place trophies and competitions. At a very young age we are placed into groups based upon our perceived abilities, and we quickly begin to understand how much or how little the world expects us to achieve. Those early 'scores' can be the catalyst for a series of actions, behaviours and unconscious beliefs, either propelling us towards the idea that we are destined for greatness or instilling doubt about our chances of success. The truth is, thankfully, much more nuanced than that. Yet even as children we have to come to terms with the feeling that the world is somehow keeping score.

If your parents believe that success involves studying, climbing the career ladder, getting married, having kids and saving for retirement, then you might have inherited some of the same ideas too. However, it's likely that you also have your own opinions and a very different vision of success for yourself. Maybe your idea of success involves the freedom to travel the world, to create something original and unique, or maybe to become rich and famous. What matters is that you realise that only you can define what success looks like at any given time throughout your life – and this knowledge can help to add meaning, value and focus to the decisions you make and the actions you choose to take.

Redefining success for yourself

Before you sit down and try to define success on your own terms, let's move back one step. First, you need to reject the traditional script that has been handed to you. If you flip some stereotypical success ideals – high social status, wealth, professional achievements and accolades – and ditch these old-school definitions, you can redefine success and create a life for yourself that's not just about ticking boxes but about finding genuine purpose and satisfaction.

We've all heard the version that says success is about 24/7 hustle and a product of hard work, determination and good luck. We're told that successful people are highly valued and respected, gain greater opportunities, earn more money and have an overall better quality of life. So, the more successful you become, the better off you'll be. It's something to be proud of and aim for. All too often, we're encouraged to follow the predefined path and climb the metaphorical

SUCCESS

ladder all the way to the top. Once we become 'successful', we've made it! We are led to believe that, at this point, life will take on new dimensions. We'll be in the VIP club along with all the other accomplished people. We can have a bigger house filled with expensive things, a wardrobe full of designer clothes, and access to the coolest places. The message that we should be striving for success is coming through loud and clear. The promise? A rewarding, fulfilling and happy life.

Let's be honest, this whole narrative is a bit . . . how do I put this? Outdated. It's as though you're handed a clichéd contract for success and just like that, you've unknowingly signed up before reading the terms and conditions. The associated costs – such as burnout, stress, perfectionism and disillusionment – later emerge as unexpected charges. A lifetime subscription to exhaustion is in the small print. The true cost of achieving success in the traditional way leaves you wondering: *Is this really it?*

Perhaps you've come across another script for success – a more contemporary interpretation that offers a shiny new 'hipster' perspective. This alternative narrative is one that champions authenticity and minimalism, and shuns personal ambition. It suggests that the traditional version of success is merely skin-deep and unfulfilling. This version is all about pursuing your passion, living in the moment and sharing 'good vibes'. There's a whispering voice telling you to break free from the pursuit of wealth and social status and find contentment regardless of the opinions and approval of others. In this reimagined portrayal, a truly successful person is defined not by the size of their bank account, the car they drive or their job title, but by the 'real' experiences they've lived (and posted about on Instagram). It's as if the pendulum has swung from one extreme to the other, and now we're being asked to abandon the traditional models of success altogether. But while this rebranding of success might seem appealing, personally I'm not convinced.

Even though this more modern interpretation of success, with its emphasis on authenticity and passion, offers a refreshing alternative to the old hustle-and-grind mentality, it still falls short in its own way. By framing success as a binary choice between material wealth and personal fulfilment, it overlooks the complexity of human nature. Life isn't simply black or white, it rarely fits neatly into one box – and success is no exception.

This newer narrative perpetuates the stereotype that chasing wealth and status inevitably leads to unhappiness and dissatisfaction. The problem? This is an oversimplification, and it fails to recognise that success is not a one-size-fits-all concept. It's deeply personal and subjective. While it's true that pursuing a passion and living a nomadic life might work for some people, it's equally true that, for others, creating a business empire and building a fortune is their definition of success. And you know what? That's perfectly okay.

By placing success into two opposing camps, there's no way of finding a middle ground that combines the traditional and modern definitions. Instead of viewing success as an either/or proposition, we should embrace the idea that it can be both/and. That is why it's essential for us to turn down the volume of everything going on around us and pay attention to our own voice. Your unique definition of success can encompass a variety of goals, personal values, aspirations and future dreams.

Instead of choosing between two polarising ideals, what if you try to find a middle ground and design your own path – one that allows you to define success in your own terms. By asking yourself a series of vital questions, you can uncover a definition of success that feels authentic to you. Here are some to get you started:

3 STEPS TO CRAFTING YOUR PERSONAL DEFINITION OF SUCCESS

Step 1: Self-reflection

Take a moment to reflect on your current understanding of success, and ask yourself the following questions:
- How have my cultural background, upbringing and past experiences shaped my definition of success?
- Are there specific words or images I associate with success?
- If ever, when have I felt pressure to conform to a certain definition of success?

> **Step 2: Challenge your assumptions**
> Challenge any preconceived notions or societal expectations you may have about success. Ask yourself:
> - Are there any traditional ideas of success that don't resonate with me?
> - Do I feel pressured to pursue success in a certain way, even if it doesn't align with my values or aspirations?
> - Are there alternative perspectives on success that I find intriguing or appealing? If so, why?
>
> **Step 3: Name it/write it down**
> Based on your reflections, craft your own definition of success using words that resonate with your values, aspirations, and vision for the future. Ask yourself:
> - How can I measure success in terms of personal fulfilment, happiness and overall well-being?
> - What does success look like in this current season of my life? How has this changed over time?
> - How can I ensure that my definition of success remains authentic to who I am and what I want, rather than being influenced by external pressures or expectations?

It takes time to peel back the layers of how our upbringing, culture and past experiences have shaped our ideas about success. There are multiple factors to consider, and it's an ongoing process. Even if you don't have answers to all of the questions outlined above, just by considering them you're taking a step in the right direction towards gaining a clear understanding of what 'success' truly means to you.

Success and happiness

Let's take a look at the complex intersection between success and happiness. Think of the three most successful people you know, and then think of the three happiest people you know. Are those three people the same? This exercise highlights a complex problem: often, we tend to fixate on achieving success, but what we really want to attain is happiness. Even if we understand that happiness and success are *not* the same thing, we still believe they are intrinsically linked.

There's a famous story that perfectly illustrates this concept. A New York businessman decided to take a vacation in a small coastal village in Mexico. One morning, as he strolled along the beach, he struck up a conversation with a fisherman. The fisherman explained that, each day, he caught just enough to support his family. He would then spend the rest of his time taking afternoon siestas and playing guitar with his friends. Dismayed by what he assumed to be a lack of ambition, the businessman advised him to fish longer hours and catch more fish. He followed this up by telling the fisherman that, with the extra profits, he could buy more boats and eventually become a wealthy businessman.

Then the fisherman asked the question: 'But what would I do then?'

The businessman replied: 'Then you could retire, live in a small coastal village, fish a little, relax, take afternoon siestas and enjoy playing guitar with your friends.'

This story highlights the importance of defining your own version of success, and understanding what brings *you* happiness and contentment. It also serves as a poignant reminder that not everyone's aspirations are the same. For some, success is about accolades and wealth; for others, it's about quality relationships and time spent enjoying a passion. What may appear a meaningless choice to one person could be a deliberate decision for another. Keep this story in mind as you attempt to write your own manifesto for success.

When you think about the most successful people and the happiest people you know, if these two groups are different, do you see a stark contrast between them or are there some obvious similarities? The people you select depend entirely on your own perception of success and happiness. Numerous studies have explored the correlation between success and happiness, and it turns out that while there can be a link between them – unfortunately, the increase of positive feeling associated with a win is only short-lived. This experience is a psychological phenomenon known as the 'hedonic treadmill' – the perpetual cycle of chasing success and experiencing temporary moments of happiness. Like a hamster on a wheel, constantly running without ever reaching a destination, the high we get from achievement can be addictive enough to keep us on this wheel of aspiration.

I'm pretty sure you can think of a time when you worked really hard for weeks or even months to achieve a goal. And I'll bet you can also remember the feeling of joy and satisfaction that followed the win. But inevitably, as the days passed, that feeling gradually started to fade. The truth is, no matter how big or small the goal, whether you passed the exam, got the promotion or bought the house, the uptick of positive emotion is only temporary. Eventually you return to your previous baseline level of contentment and start the cycle again; you set your sights on a new goal and the pattern is repeated.

But wait, is the hedonic treadmill really such a bad thing? Okay, initially the idea that we're continually striving for more and more without ever reaching a sustainable state of satisfaction sounds pretty disheartening, but there's two sides to every coin. If this is an intrinsic part of human nature, then surely there must be a reason for it. Think of it like this: from an evolutionary standpoint, feeling unsatisfied is literally what drove our ancestors to find food, explore new places and discover solutions to everyday problems. When we climbed the tree to get the berries, we felt satisfied, but only for a short time. If the satisfied feeling had remained forever, then we would never have been motivated to climb the tree again. Today, it is this same desire for progress that inspires us to innovate, learn, develop new medicines and technologies, start new businesses and improve society. One of the most positive aspects of the hedonic treadmill is that it provokes temporary motivation that continually pushes us to strive for more. It also highlights how malleable we are. Humans are the ultimate adaptation machine; we never stay the same.

When you first start strength training, lifting a twenty-kilogram weight is difficult, but over time you get stronger and you need to lift a heavier weight to get the same result. This is why it's important to centre your own values and personal definitions of success when it comes to personal growth and decision-making. The desire for 'more' isn't always a bad thing. Sometimes, more is necessary. Sometimes we desire more because we've outgrown our current situation, job or relationship. Like envy, the feeling of dissatisfaction isn't a fault in your factory settings. It's not a design flaw, but rather it's a notification letting you know that it's time for change. Dissatisfaction is not our enemy; it's a misunderstood ally. With that in mind, when you set yourself a goal, consider which type of motivation is most effective for you: the carrot or the stick?

Imagine a donkey plodding along. Its owner has placed a carrot out of reach. The donkey's gaze is fixed on the delicious carrot and so it presses forwards one step at a time, motivated by the promise of a tasty reward. This is the essence of carrot motivation. It stems from the desire for positive outcomes and taps into the psychology of hope and aspiration. If you're motivated by the carrot, you'll likely feel enthusiastic and optimistic about pursuing your goal. I've heard it's pretty common for parents to incentivise their teenagers to study for upcoming exams with the carrot of a cash reward. The higher the grade attained, the more money they pay out. Maybe an A is rewarded with £100, B is worth £50, and a C will get them £20, etc. It's easy to understand why this kind of motivation works. It feels good when you achieve the goal, especially when it provides an immediate, tangible reward.

Now, let's turn our attention to the opposite type of motivation: the stick. When the donkey is hit from behind with a stick, rather than being motivated by a reward it is being driven by fear and the desire to avoid negative consequences or pain. Does the donkey still march forwards? Well, yes, the stick motivation can drive action, but for a very different reason. (It's worth mentioning that this is a hypothetical example – no donkeys were harmed while writing this book.) There are some instances where this tough approach can work well. At school, if a child forgets to hand in their homework, they receive a detention as punishment. It's likely that many children complete their homework simply to avoid having to go to detention. The stick style of motivation is simple and effective. It can feel like fire at your heels, urging you to move forward. For many of us, a fear of failure, judgement or criticism can be a powerful motivating force, but it can also come with a constant state of stress and anxiety. When you're driven by the fear of negative consequences, you're likely to find yourself mentally exhausted and emotionally drained, and this approach is rarely sustainable in the long run.

So, when it comes to motivation, the key is to figure out which type is going to be most effective for you in each situation. Whether it's the sweet allure of the carrot or the fear of the relentless stick, both forces can be harnessed at different times to drive you towards success. Think about a goal that you're currently working towards. Can you identify the carrots – those motivating positive rewards – tempting you to continue? What is the painful stick you're keen to avoid? Make sure you know which one is driving your effort. Personally, I prefer to opt for the carrot. Eyes focused on the prize!

Success in each season: Change, challenge and growth

As we go through life, we will experience three distinct seasons: change, challenge and growth. When it comes to defining success, each of these seasons presents unique opportunities and demands, and requires a different approach to decision-making.

Seasons of change

A season of change is all about transition, transformation and a new start. This could be moving to a new place, starting a new relationship or getting a new job. This can create a whirlwind of emotions – often a blend of excitement and nervousness about starting something new. A season of change is typically a time of upheaval – but also renewal, offering a chance to reinvent ourselves and reassess our priorities. 'Success' in this season is the ability to embrace change, adapt to a new reality and seize the opportunities that it brings. A season of change requires flexibility, openness, and a willingness to be an amateur. When starting a new chapter of life, a season of change is a catalyst for growth and transformation. We need to let go of the past and look ahead to the possibilities of the future.

I've experienced many seasons of change, and each one has been significant and meaningful in its own way. In my early twenties, I became a mother and my priorities shifted in an instant. Back then, I wasn't building businesses, travelling the world or running marathons. Honestly, I had no desire to do any of those things at that time. During that season of change I was focused on one thing: learning what it meant to be a parent. For a few years, the pace of life was much slower; my days were filled with motherhood. I'd spend afternoons at the adventure park, collecting sticks in the forest or racing Lego cars around the house. Success took on a different meaning during that part of my life. My days didn't start with rushing on the London Underground to get to a meeting. I wasn't checking emails, recording podcasts or trying to come up with ideas for my next project. When I reflect on that time, I realise that I was happy, content and truly present. The idea of success for me then was simply time well spent with my son, and I made decisions that aligned with my goals at that time. It wasn't about accolades or accomplishments in the traditional sense; it was about the small victories of parenthood, like helping him take his first steps or teaching him to count.

Of course, it wasn't all fun and easy, and there were plenty of sleepless nights and tears (for baby and for me), but the good days far outweighed the bad. Then, as my son grew older and became more independent, I entered another season of change. One that involved rediscovering aspects of myself and my life that had been put on hold for a few years. I began to establish professional relationships, host events and build an online community via social media. Success in this season meant reclaiming my identity outside of being a mother, building a career, and finding balance between multiple roles and responsibilities. Through each season of significant change, we go through a sort of transformation – and with it our version of success must continually evolve too.

Seasons of challenge

A season of challenge is one that presents us with adversity, misfortune and setbacks. Whether it's coping with a loss, overcoming illness, dealing with the aftermath of a breakup or grappling with a professional failure, these unexpected moments in life hit hard. Seasons of challenge can push us to our limits and beyond. They test our resilience, perseverance and inner strength. Success in this season takes on a whole new meaning. It's not about striving for the next big

SUCCESS

milestone, or solving all of life's problems, but simply about doing something – anything, no matter how small – that you can call progress. It's about our ability to endure, adapt, and eventually overcome hardship.

While there's no such thing as the 'perfect time' to make a good decision, there are certainly times in life when it's best to avoid making any unnecessary high-stakes decisions or big life changes. It could be that we're facing a health challenge, a financial issue or a personal crisis. Seasons of challenge can feel as though we're trying to swim against the tide and we can't catch a break. When we're emotionally and mentally drained, it's nearly impossible to think clearly and be objective. Our ability to make rational, well-thought-out decisions is compromised, and we're more likely to act impulsively, make irrational choices and ignore potential future consequences. At times like this, we must remember to fall back on the rules of engagement outlined in Chapter 1.

When it feels like everything is falling apart, no doubt there will be moments when it's tempting to make some big changes, tear up the plan and start all over again. However, we should proceed with caution. There's a reason we're advised not to operate heavy machinery while tired. You see, making big life decisions during difficult times – like going through a divorce or grieving a loss – is just as ill-advised.

Getting through a season of challenge requires patience, and oftentimes you'll need help and support from friends and family. While they might not be able to offer a solution, they'll probably be willing to help you weather the storm and stand by your side, and that can make all the difference. Don't worry, I'm not going to insist that within every adversity is an important lesson – that's not my style. Instead, I'll remind you that no season, good or bad, is permanent. Nothing lasts forever. Everyone will go through a season of challenge at some point. Heartbreak, grief and failure are all a part of life. It's during seasons of challenge that our true strength is revealed, and ultimately this shapes us to become more resilient and compassionate on the other side.

Seasons of growth

Then there are seasons of growth: times of expansion and development, when we dive head-first into exploration, learning and self-discovery. We set goals and achieve them, chase our dreams and push ourselves to go further than before. Seasons of growth feel exciting and energising. They're all about thriving in our personal and professional lives. Success, in this season, is marked by progress, self-improvement, and realising our full potential.

Seasons of growth often begin with a catalyst that ignites a period of intense focus and dedication. I've observed this countless times with clients and friends. Whether they're committing to studying for an exam, training for a triathlon or launching a new business venture, setting a new goal provides structure and motivates them to clear their schedules to make room for growth.

When I first sat down and began writing this book,

initially it seemed like an insurmountable challenge, like climbing Everest. I wasn't sure how I could fit it in alongside my other commitments. It required focus, discipline and a lot of work. There's been some growing pains throughout, but the process has helped me to develop and improve as a writer.

Embracing a season of growth means stepping out of our comfort zone, daring to say 'yes', embracing new experiences and squeezing the juice out of life. It's the time to nurture our talents, cultivate relationships and seek opportunities for growth. Whether it's mastering a new skill, pursuing higher education or learning more about ourselves on a journey of self-discovery through therapy, seasons of growth propel us towards becoming our fullest selves.

Each season of change, challenge or growth has its own meaning and significance. Some will be short; others may last for years. The key is recognising and embracing the season you're currently in, and learning how to use the right decision-making tools at the right time.

Consider these three seasons and ask yourself: *Which one am I in right now?* It's also worth noticing that whenever one season is ending, you can take a moment to pause and reflect before gearing up for the next. Often, one change can be a catalyst for another, and another, then suddenly everything seems different. Even if things are moving quickly, as the sun sets on a season, ask yourself what you're going to leave behind and what you'd like to take with you into the next.

Who knows – maybe the next season of your life is going to feel like a comedy, a drama, a romance, an adventure or a tearjerker. It could be so great you'll wish you could replay it again. For better or for worse, each season shapes you. So, try to accept whatever season you're in, go with it, and remember that success may take on different forms at various stages of life.

Decision-making through different seasons

Sometimes, in our quest for massive, life-changing successes, we overlook the power of consistency and the importance of modest everyday wins. Let's narrow our focus even more and look at day-to-day success. There's a reason that following deliberate daily routines and habits increases our odds of achieving success. The small choices matter more when we make them hundreds, even thousands, of times. As discussed in Chapter 1, small, low-impact decisions, when they are repeated and enacted every day, can either propel us forward or hold us back. Too often, we focus all of our attention on life's infrequent big decisions and overlook the power of repeatable small choices.

Small actions can lead to big impacts. Financial investors call this the 'effect of compounding'. If you invest money in the stock market, as your money earns interest, you'll start to earn interest on the interest, and this leads to exponential growth over time. It's like a snowball rolling down a hill, gathering mass and momentum. This effect can also be seen in small decisions about health, learning, productivity and even mindfulness. When repeated frequently, they can have a profound impact on your life.

Ask any busy, stressed-out person about meditation and they'll probably laugh and tell you that they don't have time for that sort of thing. It might seem like sitting still for a few minutes every day won't do much – but you know what? It's actually one of the most powerful examples of the compound effect. You see, meditation is not just a woo-woo practice; it's backed by science, and it can have a profound impact on your biology.

Initially, when you start meditating for just a few minutes each day, you might not notice an immediate change. But over time, that daily practice starts to reduce stress, improve your ability to regulate emotions, and sharpen your focus. Meditation gives your body a chance to regulate the nervous system and can reduce hormones such as cortisol and adrenaline. Meditating regularly can relax your blood vessels, leading to lower blood pressure; there is increasing evidence to show that regular meditation could even slow down the ageing process and help you live longer.

You see, making the decision to meditate for a few minutes each day is investing in your mental and emotional well-being. Those small daily moments of stillness and introspection add up over time, and they can help to make you a healthier and happier person. Just like compound interest grows your savings, a daily mindfulness practice compounds your mental and emotional wealth. The beauty of this approach is its simplicity.

Repeatable low-stakes decisions can create a road map of small steps that continually lead you in the right direction. Here are some reflection prompts to help you apply some of these ideas to your life:

CORE QUESTIONS FOR EVALUATING SUCCESS IN RECENT DECISIONS

Think about a recent decision you made:
- Did you consider whether it was a high-stakes, low-stakes or no-stakes decision? How might using this framework change how you approach future choices?
- Was it the best decision for the current season of your life? Are you in a season of growth, challenge or change? What specific goals could you set to get closer to your own version of success in this season?
- Did your decision align with your long-term goals? Evaluate your daily habits and actions. How could you leverage the power of consistency and compounding?

The power of perception

Success is about perception and context. When an athlete is preparing for a 100m race, their main goal is of course to win the race by finishing in first place. Their sights are firmly set on winning the gold medal, but in sports – and in life – things don't always play out as expected. If an athlete steps up to the start line knowing that they have done all of the required preparation, and give it everything, execute every stride perfectly, cross the finish line with a new personal best but realise they have finished in second place, how would they view this race? Would they consider it a success? Well, that's for the athlete to decide for themselves. They might feel elated and celebrate their achievement; after all, they just completed a 100m sprint faster than they ever have before, and they outran six competitors. In this narrative, the race is a triumph and a success.

On the flip side, disappointment and frustration might cloud their perspective – a classic example of the negativity bias discussed in Chapter 3. They might come to the conclusion that the race was an outright failure because they didn't achieve their 'ultimate' goal of a gold medal. Their brain and perspective construct a narrative where the race becomes a missed opportunity.

Of course, it is possible – and most likely – that the athlete who finishes in second place with a personal best will feel a complex mix of emotions. They may decide that the race was a success even though they finished in second place. They may also feel the disappointment that comes with just missing the mark, alongside the motivation to improve for the next race. We can experience two competing emotions at the same time, and both can be valid and real, but how we frame the narrative of the events in our lives – the version of the story we believe to be true – is what dictates our reality, and ultimately, that is what matters most. But here's the thing, and it's a point worth underlining: I'm not suggesting we simply tell ourselves a story that feels good and give everything a positive spin; however, it is essential to find a balance between being motivated to improve and acknowledging our achievements even when they don't quite live up to our initial aspirations. Success isn't always a binary win or fail; sometimes it's ambiguous, and that's okay. Ultimately the only person who can walk the tightrope of perception and decide whether or not you've succeeded is you.

Perception also plays a part when it comes to evaluating failures. Just as the traditional model of success can be a social narrative, we can be pretty judgemental when it comes to people's failures. Let's take divorce as an example. We've been conditioned to see marriage as the ultimate success story. We're repeatedly told the fairy tale of happily ever after – a romantic narrative that is deeply ingrained and celebrated in our culture. So of course, if we find ourselves getting divorced, we get given a big fat F for failure. But when I got divorced, I didn't really agree with the narrative that a marriage that ended was therefore by default a failure. Allow me to explain further.

Why do we call divorce a 'failed marriage'? Because we've been conditioned to the idea that a successful marriage is one that lasts until death do us part, and anything short of that is seen as a defeat. But that's a flawed way of looking at things.

Firstly, it's worth remembering that getting divorced is rarely an impulsive, thoughtless decision. It's usually the result of hours, days, weeks and months of thinking, talking and tears. When two people realise that they have grown and changed, sometimes they discover that they're simply not compatible anymore. Divorce can be a courageous act of prioritising well-being and happiness over a societal ideal. In fact, staying in an unhappy or unfulfilling marriage is the real failure.

I'll admit, when I got divorced, I didn't immediately feel like opening a bottle of champagne, but I did feel liberated and, dare I say, happy. For me, divorce meant change – a chance to learn from mistakes and create a life that aligned with who I truly am. It was one of the bravest things I have ever done – the ultimate act of self-respect and self-love. My marriage may not have been a total success, but it was certainly not a total failure. So, the next time someone tells you that their marriage ended in divorce, don't respond with 'Oh I'm so sorry to hear that.' It's divorce, not death. You might congratulate them for having the strength to choose their own happiness over the social construct of a 'successful' marriage. Divorce can feel like the end of a love story, but it isn't the end of a life story. Endings and failures don't have to define you, and it doesn't really matter how anyone else perceives them either; what matters is the narrative *you* choose.

Embracing the 80 per cent rule

When it comes to measuring progress and success, I have a rule that I call '80 per cent for a pass'. Whenever I set a goal for myself, I use this to determine whether or not I have succeeded; this rule allows me to adjust for the setbacks and mistakes that are inevitable in the pursuit of any goal. The '80 per cent for a pass' rule is simple. Here's how it works.

If my goal is to write 1,000 words each day, five days a week, during the process of writing a book, that amounts to a total of 5,000 words per week. For me, the process of writing requires inspiration and creativity combined with self-discipline and focus. But life, as we all know, can throw curve balls that disrupt our well-intended plans. So, when it gets to the end of the week, I pause to assess how much I have written and discover whether or not I have achieved my weekly goal and whether I'll remain on track for my overall deadline. I've decided that if I reach 80 per cent or more of my weekly word count goal, then it's a pass. Success.

Consider this principle in a broader context. Think back to the countless exams and tests you've faced throughout your life. How often did you need a flawless 100 per cent result to pass? Almost never, right? So why is it that when we set goals, we hold ourselves to such a high standard? A perfect score would be considered almost impossible for most tests because it does not allow for a single error. Perfection is an unrealistic goal.

I've heard many people describe themselves as a perfectionist as though it were something to be proud of. When interviewing for a new job and faced with the inevitable question 'What would you say are your strengths and weaknesses?' many people will confess 'I'm a perfectionist' as a strength. They say this to a potential employer, perhaps thinking they're going to be impressed. Surely it's a good thing to strive relentlessly for the absolute best result – to go the extra mile and be willing to do 'whatever it takes' to succeed? Well, maybe not. Psychologists agree that perfectionism can cause us to put too much pressure on ourselves in the pursuit of unrealistic goals, and this ultimately leads to disappointment.

When I spoke to Thomas Curran, an assistant professor in the department of psychology and behavioural science at the London School of Economics, he told me that perfectionism is not necessarily something to celebrate. He explained that we're mistaken if we think perfectionism is positive because, at root, it's a form of deficit thinking. Meaning it comes from a sense that we're not enough or not good enough, and that we need to be perfect or at least appear to be perfect, so we're trying to conceal our shortcomings.

Perfectionists tend to measure their self-worth in relation

to their productivity and accomplishments, and are drawn to valuing 'perfect' results even when it is potentially detrimental in other areas of their life, such as personal relationships and overall well-being. Perfectionists are also more likely to lean towards the stick approach when it comes to motivation, as they're typically driven by fear of failure rather than the prospect of reward. And in addition to all of that, striving for perfection can hold us back, preventing us from starting new tasks. We get stuck in a loop of endless procrastination, and continue planning, researching, tweaking and preparing, yet we never actually start. Put simply, perfection is the enemy of progress. So, let's focus instead on getting 80 per cent for a pass.

It's important to note that this is not an endorsement of mediocrity or complacency. I'm not encouraging you to lower your expectations, or to let yourself off the hook simply because you're feeling lazy – we all know the difference between doing our best and doing the bare minimum. I'm talking here about pursuing your goals without the crushing pressure of perfection or accepting social values that do not feel authentic to you. You can give it your all, but you should also accept that you don't always need to get 10 out of 10. The '80 per cent for a pass' rule continues to be a lifeline that I can apply to many aspects of my life. For example, when I'm training for an endurance event, instead of obsessing over every gym session and every single mile in the training plan, I make sure I consistently complete 80 per cent or more. For me, success isn't about being perfect; it's about being consistently good enough. It's both satisfying and rewarding to know that I'm on track to completing my goals and defining success in my own way.

The personal ambition paradox

Last year, I was invited to deliver a talk to a room of senior employees at a technology company, in which I spoke about the importance of sharing your goals and aspirations with others. I emphasised that when we tell other people about our goals, we deepen our commitment and we become open to support and accountability from those around us. After my talk, during the Q&A, a woman in the audience asked, 'How do you have the confidence to share your biggest goals with other people?' She confessed that she often downplayed her ambition when talking to colleagues, friends and even her partner. She feared crossing the line between self-confident and overconfident. In the past she'd faced criticism for having 'too much' ambition and had been labelled as a 'workaholic'.

This question struck a chord with me, as I've come across a lot of people (usually women) with similar concerns. When it comes to confidence and personal ambition, the following questions emerge: How much is too much? When does healthy enthusiasm become an unhealthy obsession? Why are people unsupportive – or worse, critical – of those who dare to dream big?

Well, let's start by acknowledging the paradox of personal

ambition. In a culture that applauds success, it's both counter-intuitive and hypocritical that the pursuit of it often invites criticism. Why does this happen? Well, when we start chasing ambitious goals, inevitably we're challenging the status quo simply by doing something different. When we're no longer playing it safe and 'fitting in' to the boxes that others create for us, our ambitious energy can trigger all sorts of reactions, from confused expressions and questions to downright criticism. People tend to feel uncomfortable when they see someone doing things differently. They might fear change, envy our enthusiasm or simply fail to understand our vision. So, they resort to criticism.

As we discussed at the beginning of this chapter, Western cultures tend to promote a competitive environment, and this can lead to comparison and judgement. People may even go as far as painting personal ambition with a brush of guilt and shame. They might comment 'He's far too over-confident!' or 'Oh, she thinks she's better than everyone else.' As though striving to achieve anything beyond the ordinary signals self-importance and a lack of humility. However, personal ambition and the pursuit of goals and dreams are not things anyone should be criticised for. The way I see it, ambition at its core is a belief that we can create or do something impactful and that we can make a difference. It's what pushes athletes to break world records, entrepreneurs to start companies that solve problems, and scientists to create new technologies and medicines. It's driven by a sense of purpose rather than ego.

SUCCESS

We should encourage those who dare to dream big, and perhaps even look for areas in which to expand our own ambitions too. Remember that personal ambition is, well, personal. You are the only one who needs to truly believe that your goals are worth pursuing. There will be plenty of doubters and critics along the way, but that's an inevitable part of life. As Aristotle famously said, 'There is only one way to avoid criticism: do nothing, say nothing, and be nothing.' Personally, I'd rather be criticised for doing something – for trying, even if I don't succeed – than for doing nothing at all.

I refuse to feel guilty or be shamed for being ambitious, or allow other people's definitions of success to impact my decisions. To those who raise an eyebrow to personal ambition, I say, let them question, let them doubt. Do your best to ignore them and continue to go after what you want. It's important to remember that criticism, while uncomfortable, can be a sign that you're doing something worthy of recognition, even if it comes with unwanted attention. So, if you ever find yourself playing down your ambition, feeling ashamed of making decisions that align with your definition of success, or constantly fearing criticism, remember that the opinions of others, while they may be loud, are no reason to limit yourself.

Ultimately, success means different things to different people. Each individual version has been shaped by personal values, experiences and cultural perspectives. There's a push and pull between the traditional story of success and the more modern version, but the truth is, you don't have to pick one or the other – it's possible to find a blend of both. You can approach success in your own way by choosing what truly matters to you. And success can take on a new meaning in each season of life. When you acknowledge this, you can make intentional decisions with clarity and purpose.

So, as you pursue your unique version of success, remember the story of the fisherman and the businessman. It's a powerful reminder that there is no universal template for success. What you value, what brings you joy and how you define success will evolve and change throughout your life.

You are the only one who needs to truly believe that your goals are worth pursuing. There will be plenty of doubters and critics along the way, but that's an inevitable part of life.

5

IMPACT

Circles of impact, self-respect & self-sabotage, measuring the impact of decisions

Impact is the tangible outcome of the choices we make. It is a concept that we hear about often, echoed by business leaders, politicians, sports coaches and teachers, and it is usually associated with power, transformation and profound change. But you don't have to be a world leader, policymaker or CEO to have an impact, or to improve your own life and the lives of those around you. Impact isn't just about big actions; it exists on an objective scale. Your ability to create a lasting impact lies not only in grand gestures, but also in the small choices you make every day. Impact is not an abstract notion that only a handful of people are responsible for; it's a shared responsibility. Regardless of status, titles or positions in life, we each bear the responsibility for our impact on others. It's a sort of ripple effect created by the words we use, the actions we take and the values we uphold.

Have you ever considered how many people you have already impacted throughout your life? It's probably a much greater number than you realise. Think of those old friends you grew up with, the people you've dated and all the people you've ever worked with. If you can still remember their names, then they must have had some kind of impact on you, and likely vice versa. When I think back, I can still remember some of my high school teachers. They were the ones who made learning easy, who injected joy into the classroom and guided me to solve problems and overcome challenges. If you were lucky, then you might have encountered the kind of teacher who truly made an impact. The one who could see your potential, gave you a chance, boosted your self-esteem, and perhaps even impacted the trajectory of your entire life.

And what about the countless people whose names you'll never know? The person who sat beside you on a long-haul flight, the barista that made your morning latte, the fellow commuters queuing in the traffic alongside you – have you ever considered the potential impact you could have had on all of those people? Whether consciously or not, you are, in one way or another, shaping the experiences of your friends, family members, co-workers and strangers every single day. Your actions, words and behaviour all have an impact. Are you quick to uplift others and show appreciation for their efforts, or are you the first one to find fault and offer criticism when people make mistakes? It's worth remembering that the impact of the words and actions you choose can sometimes extend far beyond their immediate context and intention.

Everyday moments – such as offering your seat on a train or speaking out and standing up for what's right – have an impact, both seen and unseen. Acts of kindness, gestures of goodwill and advocating for others all hold significance. Those moments are important; those decisions matter. Regardless of your age, race, position or title, your actions, behaviour and decisions contribute to collective impact. This is a responsibility we all share, and even small actions can lead to significant change. When making decisions, whether high-stakes or low-stakes – the products you buy or the votes you cast – ask yourself: *Does this decision align with what I truly want for myself today and in the future, and who else will be impacted by my choice?*

Circles of impact: How our decisions impact others

As we go through life, our choices create a ripple effect: from the immediate impact on ourselves to the lasting influence they can have on others. The circles overleaf illustrate the multidimensional impact of our decisions. We'll go on to examine each circle in turn.

> Circle 1 – How our decisions shape our own lives
> Circle 2 – How our choices influence those closest to us
> Circle 3 – The impact we can have within our immediate communities
> Circle 4 – How we contribute to broader social dynamics.

Understanding the dynamics within these circles encourages thoughtful and intentional decision-making. Even the smallest choices we make can create impact, both seen and unseen, that extends far beyond ourselves and those around us.

The inner circle: Self-love, self-respect and self-sabotage

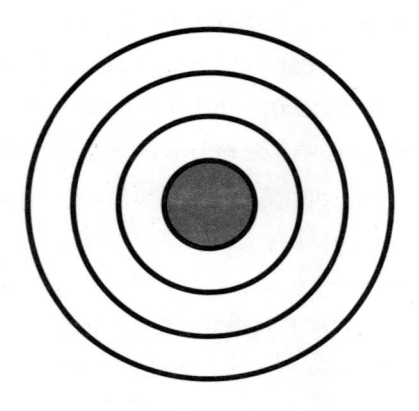

At the core of your circles of impact is the 'self'. You are the epicentre of your own life, so fundamentally the person most affected by your decisions is you. While you reap the rewards of your efforts and hard work, it's also you who gets hit hardest by the fallout of poor choices and has to face the consequences. Ultimately, this is why you must make decisions that are good for *you* and that prioritise your own happiness and well-being. If you continually make decisions that are good for everyone else and not so good for you, over time those compromises will stack up. Continually sacrificing what you want and need might seem admirable, but it's a recipe for burnout, resentment and, ultimately, unhappiness.

Before we can hope to make a positive impact on others – be it our children, our partners, our friends or the rest of the world – we have to start with ourselves. You have to learn how to make decisions with your own happiness and well-being in mind. It's important to learn how to choose YOURSELF. The starting point is to place yourself at the epicentre of the decision-making process. Now, I'm not suggesting that you just do whatever you want and forget about everyone else. That would not be useful or realistic. You're going to have to consider what other people want and need from you – your partner, children, parents and friends all matter. But here's the thing, so do you. You matter just as much as anyone else in your life.

I'm sure you've heard the words 'self-love' and 'self-compassion'. I've got to be honest, I'm reluctant to use these terms because they've become buzzwords that are used all the time in social media posts, self-help books and wellness articles. They've been watered down to the point where they now seem shallow and unimportant. Self-love and self-compassion have become synonymous with self-indulgence and self-pampering. Brands often use terms such as 'self-care' to convince us to buy expensive bath products, scented candles and monogrammed journals. Sure, I'll admit I love buying that stuff – who doesn't? However, this commercialised version misses the core of what self-love and self-compassion are all about. For me, the overlooked piece here is self-respect.

Don't get me wrong, self-love and self-compassion are not trivial; they are fundamental to our well-being. But it's self-respect that forms the foundation on which self-love and

You matter just as much as anyone else in your life.

self-compassion are built, because it establishes the standards by which we treat ourselves and allow others to treat us. Here's the thing: learning how to prioritise yourself and what you need isn't easy in a world that consistently tells you to do the opposite. I grew up in the UK in the 1990s, when the cultural norm of quietly persevering while putting on a brave face was deeply ingrained. The message to 'keep calm and carry on' was more than just a well-known slogan on a poster; it was a societal expectation. From childhood, we were taught not to make a fuss, to suppress our emotions and soldier on in the face of adversity without complaining. It's no wonder that, years later, many of us struggle to prioritise self-care and struggle with feelings of guilt when we do. Breaking free from this mindset and learning to prioritise yourself is not easy, but it's essential for your growth and overall well-being.

If the term 'self-love' feels too flimsy and uninspiring to you, then let's try to consider 'self-respect' instead. This has nothing to do with choosing a candle or having a bath; self-respect is about feeling empowered. Put simply, self-respect means having consideration and high regard for yourself. When you focus on maintaining it, you begin to act, behave and make decisions as someone you believe is worthy of respect.

When you have respect for something, you appreciate it, value it and take care of it. In contrast, when you have very little respect for something, you overlook it, and you can begin to neglect and even dislike it. Which of those descriptions most accurately describes the way you treat yourself and view the decisions that you have made in the past? I'll be the first to admit that self-compassion and self-respect haven't always come naturally to me. They are skills that I've had to learn, and that I continue to practise every day. In the past I fell into the trap of misunderstanding the concept of self-compassion, thinking it was simply a way to make excuses, let yourself off the hook and avoid accountability. I wrongly believed that embracing self-compassion would lead to complacency, laziness and a lack of motivation. (If you're a Virgo like me, then you know exactly what I'm talking about.) But you know what? I was missing the point. Self-compassion isn't about making excuses; it's about gracefully accepting that you're human and that every human is imperfect. When you make a mistake, self-compassion means responding in the same way that you would if someone you admire and respect made a mistake.

Think about it – when a person that you respect makes a mistake, what's the first thing that goes through your mind? How do you respond? Do you offer support and encouragement, or do you criticise and ridicule them? Now compare that response to the narrative that typically plays in your mind when you make a mistake yourself. The truth is, we tend to be overly critical and unforgiving towards ourselves, and we talk to ourselves in a way that is harsh and disrespectful.

Do you remember being told when you were a child to 'always treat others how you would like to be treated'? Well, I'd like you to flip that around. Start treating yourself the way you treat others. If your closest friend came to you, concerned because they'd made a mistake, how would you react? Would you offer them reassurance and encouragement? Or would you criticise and shame them? Now, imagine for a moment trying to approach your own mistakes as you would the mistakes of those you respect and love. If you're wary of self-compassion like I once was, I urge you to reconsider, because it's not about lowering your standards, it's about raising your level of self-respect.

Over time, I've learned that one of the most powerful acts of self-respect is setting and maintaining boundaries. Creating boundaries means understanding your own needs, values and limits, and then communicating them to others. It's like drawing a line in the sand and letting people know where you stand. Setting boundaries doesn't mean blocking other people's requests or creating a divide between you and them. It's about establishing your own limits and making decisions that prioritise what you need, even when that feels uncomfortable.

Imagine you have a close friend who often asks you to help them out by lending them money. It's a complicated situation to navigate; you feel awkward talking about it and find it difficult to say no. Your compassionate nature means you want to help, but over time you start to feel a mixture of resentment and frustration. You recognise the negative impact this is having on your friendship, so you decide to say no the next time they ask. Part of you feels conflicted – you keep overthinking, going back and forth, trying to justify the decision. You want to say no, but you also want to help your friend, and you feel as though you're letting them down. But here's the thing, by going against what you really need, you're choosing to let yourself down instead.

Learning how to prioritise yourself often requires making tough choices, but tough choices are an inevitable part of life. Saying no to someone's requests isn't always easy (especially when it's someone who matters to you), but it can be essential to sustaining your physical, mental and emotional well-being. If you're worried about how the other person is going to feel, then in a way that's a good thing; it means you care about them. But ultimately how *they* feel is not the most important factor in your decision.

I once heard Seth Godin talking about this topic in a conversation with Simon Sinek on the *A Bit of Optimism* podcast. Godin mentioned how saying 'no' in the moment could keep him out of trouble later. He explained that when your first instinct is to say 'yes', too often you'll find yourself overcommitted – and, inevitably, you'll have to let people down, leading to disappointment and hurt feelings later. While it's admirable to want to help others and say yes, it's also important to set realistic boundaries and expectations. When you're making a tough choice that involves setting boundaries, remember that this is not a sign of disrespect towards others; it's an act of respect for yourself.

Most importantly – when you decide to maintain boundaries, most people will accept and respect them. The only people who are likely to have a problem with you setting boundaries for yourself are the ones that benefit from you not having any. (Let that sink in.) It's worth mentioning that this behaviour isn't necessarily intentional or malicious; it could just be that they are preoccupied and focusing on their own goals, without taking into account the impact they're having on you and your well-being.

Even though we are the ones most affected by our own actions, sometimes we repeatedly make poor decisions when we 'should' know better. But why would we make decisions that undermine our own success and well-being? Well, the answer, as is so often the case, can be attributed to human nature itself: self-sabotage. It's easy to *say* what we want to do – like waking up early to go to the gym – but often our actions contradict our ambitions. We stay up too late, we have another glass of wine, we hit snooze on the alarm, and we end up skipping the gym. We make an excuse, then we find ourselves discouraged and stuck in a self-sabotaging loop of low-impact decisions that do not benefit us. This destructive pattern emerges when our present self makes decisions that undermine the goals and aspirations of our future self. The most frustrating aspect of self-sabotage is that it often occurs subconsciously.

Our brain's desire to seek short-term gratification often triumphs over long-term planning. It's difficult to resist the temptation of a quick fix and immediate gratification. And let's not forget that we are wired to seek comfort and to avoid discomfort. Sometimes, even though we know that a decision is potentially bad for us in the long run, we still choose it simply because it represents the path of least resistance. It's easier to make choices based on what we want and need in the present moment, and to avoid thinking about our long-term goals.

HOW TO OVERCOME SELF-SABOTAGE

The first step in conquering self-sabotage is awareness. You have to become familiar with the patterns, triggers and blockers that are repeatedly derailing your progress. The next step is actively working to overcome them by practising delayed gratification – the art of resisting immediate rewards in favour of a more significant long-term goal. For instance, when I sit down to start writing, I know that I need to focus and concentrate for a few hours. The end goal of the task is eventually to publish this book, but it's very easy to get distracted by more immediate rewards such as posting a video on social media and then interacting and responding to the comments from people online. I could spend an entire hour on my phone and I'll get the immediate gratification and affirmation that comes from sharing content, but I won't progress further towards the more important goal of writing and publishing a book. The obvious trigger for this self-sabotaging behaviour is my phone, with its notifications, messages and calls offering a welcome distraction from writing. So in an effort to overcome this trap, when I need to focus, I leave my phone in another room and vow to only check it after I've completed a certain amount of work.

When it comes to choosing between what we most probably *should* do versus what we actually *want* to do, too often you'll be encouraged to simply 'live in the now'. But this mantra, if unchecked, can lead to reckless and impulsive decisions. We listen to the inner voice telling us: *Go ahead, buy that expensive coat, you deserve it! You only live once.* However, when we prioritise delayed gratification, we shift our focus from seeking quick fixes and short-term rewards to pursuing meaningful goals and lasting fulfilment.

This may seem like an oversimplification, but it's important to emphasise the fact that we are often drawn to immediate comfort and pleasure – irrespective of whether pursuing it in the moment is good for our overall objectives and values. That's just the way humans are wired. But in order to progress towards our higher goals, we have to avoid the easy option and instead choose to pursue the more difficult (but ultimately more rewarding) path instead. As we've discussed throughout this book, decision-making is complex and nuanced. Will there be times when we should choose the immediate reward and prioritise fun, pleasure and joy? Absolutely! But there will also be times when it pays to resist the temptation of instant gratification, and opt for patience, discipline and sacrifice instead. The constant challenge we face is navigating that fine line between making choices based on our desires in the present moment and recognising what is best for the future.

The truth is, when we make a decision, it's essential to consider the potential impact for the self right now – as well as for our future self. Ask yourself which choices would benefit you in the moment and which choices would be best for your future goals? As we discussed in Chapter 1, sometimes we need to pause and blend what Daniel Kahneman calls systems 1 and 2 – fast and slow thinking – in order to make an effective decision. Walking this tightrope is not an easy task. The complex duality requires constant effort and commitment to our highest goals.

Before we move on to the next circle, remember – impact starts with YOU. The world will continue to demand more and more, so when making decisions that matter, do not forget to give yourself the love, compassion and respect that you deserve. By starting with yourself, you might be surprised by the positive impact of that approach – not only on your relationship with yourself, but with others too.

The second circle: Interpersonal relationships, family and friends

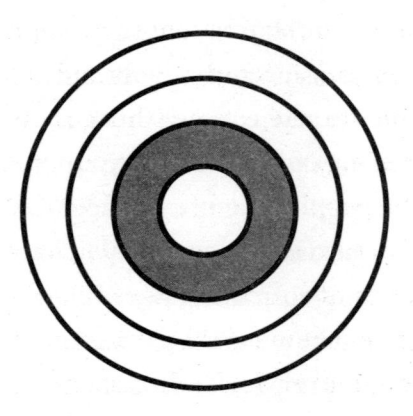

Now let's take a look at the second circle – your interpersonal relationships. These include your relationships with your partner, family and closest friends. These are the people you share your life with, the people you talk to about your hopes, dreams and fears. These relationships matter a lot; they have a profound impact on your quality of life, happiness and overall well-being. As motivational speaker Jim Rohn famously said, 'You're the average of the five people you spend the most time with.' This relates to what scientists call 'neural synchronization' – the coordinated brain activity of multiple people. In other words, when two friends with similar interests spend time together, their brain patterns can begin to synchronise. Who are the five people you spend the most time with? How do you impact each other's ideas, actions and behaviour?

The quality of our relationships can impact the overall quality of our lives. Healthy, functional interpersonal relationships are connections based on mutual respect, trust and a genuine understanding of each other. These are relationships that grant you the freedom to be your raw unfiltered self and express your ideas, thoughts and emotions without fear of judgement or rejection. Think about the people in your life that bring out the best in you – the ones you can depend on, the people who lift you up. Nurture those connections, and in turn they'll nurture you back.

The benefits of nurturing these important interpersonal connections are multilayered. Essentially, we are wired for connection, and should try to spend as much time as possible with the people that matter to us. We need to share our joy, celebrate each other's successes, and show up for one another during challenging times. We should nurture those connections like our lives depend on it. Because – well, they sort of do. Research consistently shows that good interpersonal relationships contribute positively to our physical health as well as our emotional well-being. Having a strong social network has been linked to lower rates of chronic diseases, improved immunity, and faster recovery from illness. On the flip side, loneliness and social isolation have detrimental effects on our biology and health. Therefore it's crucial that we invest time and effort into cultivating and maintaining meaningful relationships.

With each relationship, whether it's with a romantic partner, a close friend or a family member, remember that it's a two-way street. Both people must take an active role and participate in creating and sustaining the relationship. Imagine the following scenario: you've recently taken on a big work commitment at the same time as signing up for a marathon, and you've also agreed to babysit your friend's kids in a few weeks' time. (I've found myself in a similar situation to this before, because I'm both an optimist and a recovering people-pleaser.) It doesn't take long for you to realise that it's not feasible to give each one of these commitments the time and energy that it deserves – so now, my friend, you are overcommitted. Sure, your enthusiasm was well intended, but sadly that's not enough to make the impossible possible. Your colleagues are depending on you to lead the project, but you're stretched thin – and your inability to deliver understandably causes frustration and stress for you and your co-workers. Then the majority of your time before and after work is taken up with training runs and gym sessions as you prepare for the marathon. By the time it comes to babysitting, you're exhausted and resentful that you agreed to do it in the first place, so now you're trying to find a way to get out of it.

Unintentionally, you've become someone who lets people down and fails to follow through on commitments. Naturally, you're beating yourself up for getting yourself into this situation. It's a sobering truth that your choices, both wise and regrettable, impact those around you. Everyone can be forgiven for falling into the overcommitment trap from time to time, but if the habit of saying 'yes' persists when 'no' should prevail, you'll repeat the cycle and eventually your friends and family will no longer feel as though they can rely on you.

When making decisions that impact your closest family and friends, make sure you consider the knock-on effect your choices might be having on them. If you're a repeat offender who often finds yourself overcommitted, return to Chapter 1 and the section on the third rule of engagement: make it simple. Assess, evaluate and then eliminate. Be ruthless, and remember that every decision involves trade-offs and compromises.

DECISION-MAKING THROUGH CONFLICT

Okay, so relationships are important, we know that, but they're not always easy. The truth is, in any relationship, conflicts are as inevitable as taxes and bad hair days. We can't avoid them, but how we choose to handle conflict is what counts.

When it comes to resolving fallouts with loved ones, communication, patience and sometimes a sense of humour can be helpful. You've probably heard that when it comes to building great relationships, communication is key. Typically, people think that being a good communicator means being good at talking, but in fact it's much more important to be good at listening. Effective communication means actively listening and being open to the other person's viewpoint. If you want to get better at listening, start by asking more questions. As you listen to the responses, resist the urge to interrupt, be thoughtful and don't respond quickly.

When I spoke to Charles Duhigg, author of *Supercommunicators*, about how to improve communication in our interpersonal relationships, he shared this vital insight with me: 'Asking questions is key. And we know that supercommunicators ask ten to twenty times as many questions as the average person . . . The easiest way for us to show that we're listening is to do something called "looping for understanding". This is where we ask a question and then repeat back what we heard the person say in our own words, then we ask them if we got it right. The reason this is so powerful is because it proves to the other person that we're actually listening to them.' I've practised looping for understanding myself and found it incredibly helpful – especially in the heat of a disagreement, when it's important for both parties to feel as though their perspective is being heard and understood.

IMPACT

When conflicts arise, as they inevitably will in personal relationships, try to approach them with empathy and a genuine desire to resolve things. It's not about winning or losing, or who's right and who's wrong. Often it's about finding the middle ground, compromising when necessary, and trying to reach a solution that everyone can live with. In the middle of a disagreement, take a pause and ask yourself: *Am I trying to be effective or am I trying to be right?* Being effective means actively trying to make progress and acting in a way that shows that you are trying to solve the problem. Whereas trying to prove that you're right is often far less productive. Lastly, remember that a great relationship is not defined by the absence of conflict, but by how you choose to approach and overcome it when it happens.

One of the most complex decisions that we face in relationships is the decision to forgive. Forgiveness is often considered a virtue, as taught by spiritual leaders, teachers and gurus – but like so many things in life, it's much harder to practise than it is to preach. The decision to forgive is not always straightforward. It can be a long and arduous journey. For many of us, it is often deeply personal, as it involves confronting negative emotions related to our experiences. Sometimes we might find ourselves in a situation where forgiveness doesn't feel like the right choice – and you know what? That's okay. Even though we might feel pressured to simply forgive and forget as this can be empowering, so too can be the decision to withhold forgiveness when it's not genuinely felt or deserved. This doesn't mean that we remain angry or vindictive – it can simply be a conscious choice that reinforces our boundaries and a refusal to tolerate further harm.

Forgiveness, as I see it, is not a singular moment but rather a process. A complex, messy and sometimes even infuriating process that takes time. At first glance, it might seem like a concession, a surrender or even a sign of weakness. Like you're giving in and letting them off the hook. But here's the thing – forgiveness is not about the other person; it's about you. It can be an act of strength. When you choose to forgive, you release the grip of anger and resentment that can weigh you down. It's liberating! Even if the person who wronged you is unaware or unapologetic, forgiveness can still be a valuable process for your own emotional well-being. Personally, I'd rather choose to forgive than allow someone else's past actions to cast a shadow over my present and my future. But whether we choose to forgive or not, what matters *most* is that we make a choice and find a way forward that feels right for us.

EVALUATING YOUR RELATIONSHIPS

A relationship cannot exist solely due to a shared history. Just because someone has been a part of your life in the past does not automatically qualify them to be a part of your life at present or in the future. If there's someone you keep avoiding or you find yourself making excuses every time they try to connect, it's worth asking some important questions.

Choosing to end a relationship, whether it's with a friend, a family member or a romantic partner, can be one of the most difficult decisions you'll ever have to make. I find it's helpful to consider whether a friendship or relationship has a shared past, valuable present and a potential future.

A shared past can provide the foundation for a relationship, offering memories, experiences and an understanding that can deepen the connection between individuals. However, the past alone cannot sustain a relationship indefinitely. Relationships need to evolve and grow as you do, and they need to be based on mutual respect, trust and shared values. If you find yourself unsure about whether or not you are still connected with someone in your life, it's worth remembering that a relationship that is valuable in the present is one that currently contributes in a meaningful way and enriches your life. You should be supportive of each other's goals and aspirations. Both people in the relationship will feel understood and appreciated. You have mutual expectations and enjoy the time you spend together.

It's equally important to consider the potential future of a relationship. One that may have shared goals and visions for the future. One where you both envision continued growth and mutual support. While the future is uncertain, you can invest time and energy into this relationship with a long-term mindset.

If you feel you might be facing the breakdown of a relationship, ask yourself these questions:

- Does your relationship have a shared past, a valuable present and/or a potential future?

....

....

....

....

- If you used to enjoy spending time together, when and why did that change?

....

....

....

....

- Do you share similar values? And if not, is there room for compromise?

....

IMPACT

....

....

....

- Do you feel as though you can fully be yourself when you're with this person, or is it necessary to change your behaviour to accommodate them?

....

....

....

....

- How do they respond or react when you're experiencing a difficult and challenging time?

....

....

....

....

- How do they respond or react when you're experiencing happiness and joy?

....

....

....

....

- Are the expectations each of you have of the relationship aligned?

....

....

....

....

Typically, when we answer these kinds of questions honestly, it becomes clear whether we should attempt to sustain the relationship. Sometimes we will find we need to put in the work to repair and restore a once-wonderful relationship to its former glory. One practical way to start rebuilding a relationship is by confronting any issues, and having the difficult conversation even if it involves conflict. Being honest and vulnerable isn't easy, but it's necessary in order to build meaningful connections. Don't settle for dishonest harmony in your life because you're avoiding honest conversations and necessary conflict. Keep in mind that rebuilding a relationship takes time, patience and effort, but eventually it will be stronger as a result.

Sometimes, however, there will be times when we must accept that, for one reason or another, this season has ended and you're each heading down very different paths. This is the time to trust your gut. If the feeling is mutual, then there won't be any guilt or shame. You might feel a sense of sadness that the relationship has ended, or you might just feel relieved – either way, it's better for both of you to spend your limited time and energy elsewhere.

Letting such relationships go allows you to focus your attention and love on the people who matter most. As you think about the interpersonal connections within this circle, remember that relationships aren't static; they're dynamic, evolving and complex entities that require maintenance and occasional recalibration.

The third circle: Your community

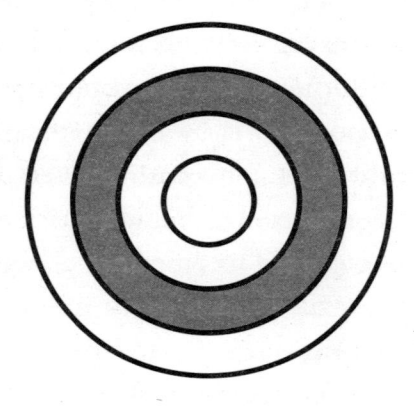

Moving outward, we enter a broader circle of impact. This includes your wider community, professional network and social acquaintances. Here, your impact might not be as direct, but it's no less significant. Within this broader circle, the quality of your relationships plays an important role. For instance, maintaining strong work friendships can significantly improve our experience at work. Research supports this notion; a study of 1,052 companies across the UK revealed compelling data – 57 per cent of employees reported that having a 'best friend' at work made their job more enjoyable, 22 per cent felt it increased their productivity, and 12 per cent were less likely to leave the company. These findings underscore how our interactions within our professional network directly impact our well-being and decision-making.

Whether consciously or unconsciously, we are impacting

those around us, and we also absorb their attitudes and ideas. Sure, we like to think that we're fiercely independent – immune to the influence of other people's opinions and the constant stream of media, marketing and advertisements that surrounds us. But the truth is, human beings are like sponges, and we're soaking up the world around us. It's seemingly impossible to avoid. But maybe this doesn't have to be a bad thing – if we are deliberate about who and what is influencing us, maybe we can use this to our advantage. You see, we're social creatures, and we tend to adopt similar attitudes and behaviours to those of the people we spend the most time with. Our brains are designed to pick up on the moods and ideas of others. When we walk into a room, often we will immediately sense the tone and the vibe. It's like there's an unwritten code of conduct. Unconsciously, we respond in a way that's appropriate.

And it's not just the people we spend time with. It's the media we consume on a regular basis, the brands we buy and the ads we see. They all influence our decision-making, shaping our desires and telling us what's cool and what's not. Consumerism makes us want the newest tech gadgets, the most recent fashion and the most Instagram-worthy experiences. If you think you're immune to all those social media ads and shop front displays, think again. These messages about 'must haves' and the latest trends seep into the subconscious.

This is why brands will pay upwards of $5 million for a thirty-second advert during half-time at the Super Bowl. This willingness to spend so much money on a single advert lasting less than a minute demonstrates the effectiveness of TV adverts. It's worth noting that Super Bowl commercials are not only seen by millions of viewers during the game, but are also viewed and shared on social media and in the news – extending the reach and impact further. The truth is, marketing works because brands understand human behaviour. They know that we all feel FOMO (the fear of missing out) and that we want to look and feel good, so we'll spend money on products that promise to make us happier and appear younger, sexier, healthier, etc.

We're wading through a sea of influence and we can't escape it – but what can we do about it? Well, firstly, just acknowledge it and recognise that your brain is not an impenetrable fortress. You're human, and therefore you're being influenced by your surroundings all the time. One of my personal decisions and a key bit of advice is to consume media that adds value to your life and that teaches you something new. Personally, I listen to audiobooks and podcasts every day; it's like a gym session for the mind. I also follow people on social media who are sharing information that is useful and who provide an alternative perspective on the world. And I subscribe to news channels that share impartial, unbiased news (at least, that's the aim). It's not always easy to differentiate fact from fiction – especially because, as mentioned in Chapter 1, online algorithms tend to prioritise clicks and controversy over truth and reality. So, you have to be discerning about what you consume and seek out sources you can trust.

Here are a few key questions that can help you to make better decisions when it comes to how you choose to engage with the world at large:

1. **What media sources do I consume regularly, and how do they shape my world view?** *Be mindful of the information and perspectives you listen to. Seek diverse perspectives and avoid creating echo chambers that reinforce your own biases.*

2. **How do the brands and adverts that I see online impact my purchasing decisions?** *For example, consider whether you are buying items that you genuinely want and need.*

3. **What role is 'external influence' playing in the decision-making process?** *Reflect on whether you're making certain choices simply because they're what others expect or want you to do, even if they're not what you really want.*

Answering these questions honestly can help you gain a clearer understanding of the true impact of external influences, and how everything from scrolling online to friendship dynamics can shape who you are, what you want and what you care about.

Social media is one way to amplify your impact, and it doesn't matter how many followers or connections you have. If you regularly share useful articles, tips and events that you're interested in, other people can benefit from these too. Unbeknownst to you, when a distant acquaintance comes across one of your posts and is inspired to share it with their network, this creates a ripple effect that extends far beyond your immediate connections. I experienced this first-hand when my first book, *Power Hour*, was released. Seeing LinkedIn posts, Tweets and Instagram recommendations from people across the globe was both humbling and heart-warming. I even read a post about a book club in Korea that was reading it as their 'Book of the Month'. You just never know how far and wide your impact can go!

The outer circle: A global scale

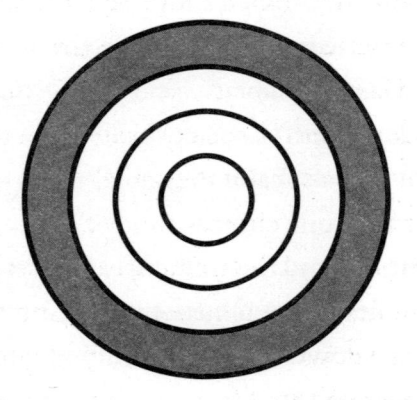

The outer circle represents global impact. Your influence here may seem distant and intangible, but it's very real. It's easy to fall into the trap of thinking, *What can one person possibly*

do? But this is a defeatist attitude that holds us back from taking action. Your choices as a consumer, voter, traveller and global citizen can have a broader reach and greater impact than you might realise. Prioritising sustainability by choosing eco-friendly products, reducing waste and advocating for sustainable practices can significantly impact our planet. Your purchasing decisions can influence brands to adopt responsible practices, therefore creating a greener world and a positive impact for future generations.

This illustrates how individual actions contribute to collective solutions. It is yet another example of how everyday low-stakes decisions that are seemingly inconsequential in the present moment can lead to a meaningful contribution over time. When millions of people make similar choices, it's a significant shift in behaviour and a catalyst for change in industry practices. We each have the power to make a profound and lasting change.

The Greek proverb 'A society grows great when old men plant trees in whose shade they shall never sit' is a beautiful reminder that our choices today can create impact for future generations and can influence the lives of people we'll never meet. At first this might seem daunting, but rather than feeling weighed down by the enormity of global challenges, we should be empowered to act with purpose and foresight, and encouraged to consider the long-term impact of our decisions and actions. This mindset can inspire us to think beyond ourselves and look to a more optimistic and hopeful future.

Kindness without sacrifice

There's a misconception that acts of kindness, generosity and making a difference require grand gestures, monumental effort and self-sacrifice. However, we can have a positive impact on others in a meaningful way without being a martyr. For example: Let's say you and I are going out for a long walk together on a sweltering hot day. You've thought ahead and packed two bottles of ice-cold water in your bag. As we make our way along the trail, the sun beating down, the heat becomes intense. About an hour in, I realise that I've made a rookie mistake – I've forgotten to bring any water and we're not even halfway there yet. In that moment, you step in with a simple yet generous act of kindness. You offer to share your water with me. Now we have one bottle of water each, ensuring we can complete the hike together. This act is relatively small, and you might say anyone would be willing to do this. After all, you didn't have to go thirsty in order to help me. It's an act of kindness in its simplest form – without any burden of self-sacrifice.

But now let's consider a slightly different version of the same story. What if you had packed only one bottle of water? In this case, giving me your water, even if it means you going without, is another level of kindness – a genuine act of self-sacrifice. Throughout our lives there will no doubt be situations that require true self-sacrifice. We may choose to give up our time, resources or even personal goals and desires to benefit others. Typically, such a decision comes from a sense of duty, love or commitment, and it's significant because we're willingly prioritising the needs of others over our own. Yet let's not underestimate the power of the small acts of kindness that do not require us to go without. They're just as valuable and important. You don't have to wait for an epic moment to be kind and have an impact. You can choose to make decisions that create a positive impact for others without self-sacrifice.

If you see someone struggling with something small, like carrying a heavy bag up a flight of stairs at the airport, offer to help. It's a small gesture that could make a big difference. When you know a friend who is going through a tough time, take a few minutes to send a text, an email or a card to let them know you're thinking about them. Your words of encouragement and emotional support will help them more than you know.

Psychotherapist Esther Perel says 'We're living in a time of artificial intimacy.' We have a thousand friends online but nobody to feed our cat when we go on holiday. We have friends without experiencing true friendship. Real connections are more important than ever. How can you connect more of the people that you know together? Could you send an email to recommend someone for a job? Could you invite some friends that don't yet know each other to dinner who you think would get along well? It might only take a few minutes to connect two people, and you never know the impact that introduction could have. They could decide to launch a business together. They could get married and even have kids. Okay, I'm getting carried away, but you get the point.

How do we measure the impact of our decisions?

When someone asks 'What impact will this have?' initially it can be difficult to give them a definitive answer. You'll need to know: Which factors are you measuring? What is the time frame? Who will be impacted?

Over the last few years, I've worked with a variety of charities and community-interest companies that are working to improve the lives of disadvantaged young people living in London. Each year, these organisations create an impact report to demonstrate how the money from donations and sponsorship they've received is being used to impact the lives of those who need it. Charities, after all, exist to make a positive difference in the world, so these impact reports are more than just a formality, they are important for several reasons. Firstly, the report is like a receipt of all the good work the organisation has done – the tangible evidence and proof that they're making a real difference in the lives of individuals, communities and causes. Next, there's the power of data. By collecting and analysing data, charities can clearly see which programmes and initiatives are working well and which need to be redesigned. Having this information helps the charity to deliver on their overall mission and keeps everyone on track. And lastly, impact reports can be a powerful tool for motivating volunteers and donors. When people see the real-life impact they're making, it fuels their commitment and is a reminder that their hard work and generosity is contributing to something bigger.

Recently, I was reading through an impressive impact report and it got me thinking. What if we applied a similar framework to our own lives? What if we could create our own personal impact report to track our progress and effectiveness, and to measure the impact of our decisions? It's an idea worth exploring. So, let's take a look at what a typical impact report would include, and how you could apply this to your daily life.

ORGANISATIONAL MODEL FOR MEASURING IMPACT

1. **Mission and goals**
   A clear outline of the mission and the specific goals that they aim to achieve. For example – to provide work experience programmes and opportunities to young people who are interested in pursuing a career in the creative industries.

2. **Collecting and measuring data**
   Using metrics to track progress and measure impact, for example how many young people completed a work experience programme this year and what percentage of them were offered employment as a result.

3. **Stories and testimonials**
   Impact reports often feature stories and testimonials from beneficiaries. These personal anecdotes provide real-life examples of the charity's work.

4. **Future plans**
   Outlining future plans and how they intend to continue making a difference.

Without making it overly complicated, let's take a page from this playbook and apply it to our own lives. Imagine creating your own report to measure the real impact of your decisions.

PERSONAL MODEL FOR MEASURING IMPACT

1. **Your mission and your goals**
   What are some of your current goals? Remember to set goals that are aligned with your own values and are appropriate for your current season (change, challenge or growth). Make sure the goals are specific, tangible and have clear action points. For example: *Get a promotion at work within the next 12 months / Save £600 for a city break this summer / Improve fitness by running three times each week.*

2. **Collecting and measuring data**

   Now, this step is critical: measure the impact of your decisions towards achieving these goals. For instance, if you decide to go to bed early instead of staying up late, track how it affects your productivity, mood and energy levels the next day. Is there a correlation between the decision to go to bed early and the ability to get up and run in the morning? Track patterns in the data over time to identify trends.

3. **Stories and testimonials**

   Talk to friends and/or your partner about some recent decisions and their subsequent effects. Share your experiences honestly and listen to theirs. Real experiences provide us with valuable insights and support. It's important to mention this is not an opportunity to outsource your decision-making to others. It's okay to ask for advice, but ultimately you have to be happy with the decision you're making.

4. **Future plans**

   Define the impact you want to have in the long run. When you assess and reflect on your impact report, be willing to make adjustments to your decision-making if/when necessary.

DECISIONS THAT MATTER

This exercise becomes relevant and useful when we see an overview of the results, so carve out some time to sit down with a notebook and a coffee to assess and measure the impact of your decisions. For sustained growth and progress, this could be a weekly or monthly reflection. Here's an example of a personal impact report:

PERSONAL IMPACT REPORT

Goal: Improve health
Decision: Go to bed early.
Short-term impact: Missing out on watching TV. Getting more sleep. Waking up with more energy, better mood, more time for morning routine and exercise.
Long-term impact: Improved overall fitness and health.

Goal: Prioritise important relationships
Decision: Turn off my phone on Sundays.
Short-term impact: Less distraction, feeling more engaged and present.
Long-term impact: Enhanced connection to family and friends, better mental health.

Goal: Career progression
Decision: Volunteer to lead a challenging project at work.

> **Short-term impact**: Increased responsibility and a feeling of high pressure to deliver.
> **Long-term impact:** Skill development, career advancement, increased income.

I know this might seem a bit formal, but you might be surprised by how effective an exercise like this can be. By creating a personal report, you're better able to measure the true impact of your decisions.

Over time, you'll start to become much more aware of your choices and their short-term and long-term consequences. Just as organisations use impact reports to demonstrate their effectiveness, you can use this approach to live a more intentional life. Creating a personal impact report can motivate you to continue making good decisions as you're able to see the positive outcomes of your choices. It can also prevent you from repeating poor decisions that have negative knock-on effects. It's a subtle but powerful way to measure the true impact of your decisions.

In conclusion, the concept of impact is significant when we think about the consequences of our decisions, both for ourselves and those around us. From low-stakes everyday choices to less frequent high-stakes decisions, impact isn't just an abstract idea, it's real and tangible. The ripple effect of our decisions can extend outwards in ways we might not even anticipate. The words we say and the actions we take create a cycle of cause and effect. Rosa Parks believed that 'one person can change the world'. And when one person believes they can have an impact, it can be a catalyst for bold decisive action. So, let's take ownership of our choices and realise the power we have to impact others and make change – no matter how big or small.

6

MAKING DECISIONS IN THE REAL WORLD

*Training your decision-making muscle,
how to use a decision-making matrix*

Ever find yourself reading the final chapter of a book that promised to transform your entire life, feeling underwhelmed and relatively un-transformed? Let's be real for a moment – flipping through these pages won't magically overhaul your life. Why? Because theory alone isn't going to cut it. It's the practice, the repetition and the tough real-world experience that will truly hone your decision-making skills. Let's take running, for instance. You could spend hours studying the science of endurance, analysing race strategies and binge-watching highlight reels of legendary runners. Would any of this make you a better runner? Sure, you might pick up a tip or two, but the truth is, the one thing that is pretty much guaranteed to make a difference is actually running. No amount of contemplation or planning can ever replace the fundamental act of lacing up your shoes, stepping out the door and going for a run.

A central mantra for improving just about anything in life is: *Reading is good, doing is better.* That's where true progress happens. Training your decision-making muscle is just like training any other muscle, so let's get to it.

We've studied the art and science of decision-making as well as the importance of understanding our values, carving out space for joy, redefining success and making an impact – all the while remembering to differentiate between decisions that matter and those that don't. So now, let's focus on putting the ideas shared in this book into action in the real world. As outlined in the introduction, it's important to pause and consider what that looks like for many of us today. Spoiler alert: living in the modern world is similar to riding a hypersonic rollercoaster without a seatbelt. It's fast, exciting and scary, and you're just doing your best to hold on!

The influence of external conditions

Try to envision the ideal environment for decision-making. Close your eyes and dream up a space that's whatever you like. I'm picturing a calm, quiet and open space with comfortable seating, beautiful green plants, and daylight pouring in through expansive windows. But if I really wanted to ensure this space was optimised for complex thinking, problem-solving and creativity, I'd go a step further. I'd dial up the ambience by setting the temperature to between 20 and 22 degrees Celsius – not too hot, not too cold; the perfect balance to remain comfortable and focused. Next, I'd add soundproofing to eliminate any distractions and ensure a quiet environment for concentration. I might even put up some inspiring artwork on the walls and the ceiling. Aesthetic elements can

Reading is good, doing is better. That's where true progress happens. Training your decision-making muscle is just like training any other muscle.

inspire creativity, enhance positive mood and foster innovative thinking. Finally, I'd make sure the space was private so as to create a sense of confidentiality and security, allowing for open and honest conversations without interruptions.

Now, contrast this with an alternative environment – one that makes clear thinking a lot more challenging. I'm picturing a chaotic, loud, crowded space filled with clutter and mess. The lighting and temperature are constantly changing, making it difficult to get comfortable. There's very little natural light, no plants and no artwork on the walls. This space is hectic and busy, with constant noise, distractions and interruptions. People are coming in and out, and many of them are talking loudly, making demands and asking questions. There's no sense of privacy, boundaries or personal space. This environment makes creativity, concentration and problem-solving virtually impossible. Why? Because there's no respite from the sensory overload – just an endless stream of stressors, each vying for your attention and draining your mental reserves.

So, which environment would you choose to step into when faced with an important decision? And more importantly, which one most accurately mirrors your current state of mind?

The thing is, for most of us living in the modern world, chaos and divided attention are the new normal. Our state of mind is continually influenced by a variety of external factors. One of the most pervasive and impactful of them all is stress. On a typical morning, in the middle of another

Zoom meeting with your boss, you may notice your inbox pinging every few minutes, hear your dog barking in the background, and then remember an important message you saw yesterday but forgot to respond to. Not exactly the ideal setting for clear-headed thinking, right? This combination of mental clutter, distraction and sensory overload is the perfect recipe for stress. It's no wonder you can't even decide what to eat for lunch most days.

Put simply, stress is the body's response to perceived threats or challenges. Our brains are finely tuned and hard-wired to notice and respond to whatever is going on around us. But here's the thing: while our ancestors faced immediate dangers such as hungry predators, our modern lives, filled as they are with constant distractions, subject us to prolonged relentless stressors. They come up constantly in the form of notifications, and this creates a number of physiological responses that can sabotage our ability to think clearly.

In a heightened state of stress, the brain releases cortisol and adrenaline. These hormones are designed to make us engage and act quickly – we try to respond to everything that is demanding our attention. In this state, the sympathetic nervous system becomes the primary operating system. This is commonly referred to as our 'fight or flight' response. It's like flicking a switch in the brain that tells the body to act now and think later. The result? Rationality takes a back seat as our primal instincts kick into overdrive. In this state we're not making thoughtful decisions, we're reacting on autopilot.

Here's a sobering thought: prolonged stress can have a

similar effect on our brains to alcohol. Ever notice how after drinking a few glasses of wine, you're less concerned about tomorrow's problems? Well, in part, this is because our ability to think ahead and weigh up the future consequences of our actions is being suppressed. Elevated cortisol levels, a signature of chronic stress, can impact the brain's control centre – the prefrontal cortex – the area of the brain which is responsible for future planning, decision-making and impulse control. Quite simply, when we're attempting to make decisions while under the influence of stress, we might as well be making decisions while drunk. Pretty scary, right?

A recent study linked excessive screen time – in particular, viewing social media content – to increased levels of cortisol. This is evidence that our addiction to scrolling our feeds could be slowly eroding our mental well-being and reducing our ability to make decisions. When we're enduring chronic stress, the qualities that we need for effective decision-making – such as clarity, foresight and objectivity – become much harder to access. Tasks that once seemed manageable suddenly feel daunting, and contrary to popular belief, stress doesn't always lead to overwhelm and indecision. In fact, it often pushes us towards impulsive action. Under the influence of stress, we are less equipped to uphold boundaries and much more likely to be derailed by quick fixes and short-term solutions. Stress can leave us feeling drained and defeated, making it all too easy to give in to the demands of others so as to avoid conflict and conserve precious energy.

I'm pretty sure this is why parents of toddlers often give in and cave to the outrageous demands of their two-year-olds. A combination of stress and tiredness makes it challenging for parents to engage in negotiation and a battle of wills, especially in the middle of the night. Exhausted and frazzled, they surrender to the tyrannical toddler. (We've all been there.) However, it's not all bad news, I promise. There are plenty of things we can do (detailed later in this chapter) to mitigate the effects of stress and reclaim our decision-making power – even in the most demanding circumstances.

The right amount at the right time

It's worth noting that not all stress is bad. For years, we've been told that stress is the culprit responsible for poor sleep, poor health, depression, anxiety, wrinkles and just about every other thing we want to avoid. It's true that too much stress can cause problems, but a manageable amount of stress can be beneficial. Yes, that's right, stress isn't always the bad guy. For some, stress can be a catalyst for peak performance. It can work as the motivational stick to help them towards their goals. The right amount at the right time can sharpen focus, enhance motivation and initiate an adaptive response to challenges. In other words – when the pressure's on, we can rise to the occasion.

An actor on stage in front of a live audience can channel this kind of stress-induced energy to improve their performance. The buzz of adrenaline can turn a good show into an unforgettable one. In this way, stress is not a hindrance; it's a tool that enhances success.

I've always been the kind of person who responds well to deadlines and a healthy dose of pressure. In the last few minutes before I walk on stage to deliver a presentation, I feel a recognisable surge of adrenaline and I become hyper-focused. In that moment, the pressure isn't a burden, it's a catalyst, I know it enables me to perform at my best. Sure, I feel nervous, but I've learned to reframe those feelings of heightened pressure as enhancing, rather than experiencing them as stressful and debilitating.

When high-pressure moments are an isolated point of peak stress, they can help us to achieve success, but it's crucial to strike a balance. It's well understood that prolonged excessive stress can tip the scales in the opposite direction, resulting in disastrous effects. The key here is to moderate the duration and the frequency of periods of stress. Even the most elite athletes know that you can't sustain a maximum level of intensity day in and day out – that's a recipe for burnout, not success.

How much stress is too much?

In 1967, psychiatrists Thomas Holmes and Richard Rahe developed the Holmes and Rahe stress scale, which aims to quantify the impact of major life events on stress levels. It involves assigning a score from 1 to 100 – which they called 'life-change units' (LCUs) – to various common life events based on their perceived stressfulness. For example, getting married (50), the death of a close family member (63), moving house (20), graduating from school (26), taking out a loan (17), children leaving home (29), etc. Participants in the original study were asked to indicate which of these life events they had experienced within a twelve-month time frame, and their scores were totalled to determine their overall stress level. People who scored 150 points or more had a 50 per cent chance of experiencing stress-related health problems.

Holmes and Rahe's research laid the groundwork for understanding the relationship between life events and stress, highlighting that major life changes – whether positive or negative – can significantly contribute to stress. More importantly, their findings also showed that continual stressors can later lead to illness.

When you decide to make a big life change – such as quitting your job after months of contemplation – that one decision often becomes a catalyst for another change, and another and another. Before long, you're moving out of your flat, becoming a vegan and getting a dog. Now, this isn't necessarily a bad thing; sometimes change is needed and beneficial. However, before you decide to make significant life changes, considering the insights from the Holmes and Rahe stress scale study can be valuable.

Firstly, let's acknowledge that all major life changes, whether positive or negative, will bring about some stress. It seems you can't have one without the other. Even just understanding that these changes impact our stress levels allows us to be more prepared and better manage our health and decision-making during transition periods.

Well, what does this mean in practice? It's usually a good idea to assess your current stress levels, the season you're in, and reflect on recent life events to gauge your overall capacity before making significant life changes. While some changes may have positive outcomes in the long run, they may also require short-term sacrifices and pressure. As discussed in Chapter 4, it's useful to assess whether you have the resources and support to navigate the transition effectively right now – and to consider seeking additional support such as therapy or coaching.

So, how can we reclaim our ability to make decisions in the face of stress? Fear not, I'm not going to tell you simply to avoid stress. I live in the real world, and that is vague and unrealistic advice. Instead, here are some workable solutions. Once you are armed with awareness and these practical coping strategies, you can reclaim control and make a shift from chaos to calm.

Stress strategies

1. Single-tasking

Repeat after me: 'Multitasking is a myth.' Most of the time, when we think we're multitasking, what we're actually doing is task switching. Constantly jumping from one task to another is inefficient at best; and let's not forget that overstimulation creates additional stress for both mind and body. Instead, focus on doing one task at a time.

Single-tasking allows your brain to devote all of its resources and attention to the job at hand. Have you ever lowered the music volume all the way down in the car to concentrate on parking? If so, you're not alone. Essentially, single-tasking isn't just about increasing productivity; you're turning down distraction and dialling up concentration. Perhaps one of the most important reasons to give it a go is to experience and enjoy life's moments a little more.

Last year I noticed that I'd taken James Clear's brilliant concept 'habit stacking' a bit too far. If you're not familiar with the concept, here's a simple explanation. The idea is to take an existing daily habit – like brushing your teeth or making a coffee – and stack a new behaviour on top of it. Think of it as creating a domino effect for positive change. For example, if your aim is to read more, you could stack reading for ten minutes on top of your daily coffee-making. Want to keep up to date with global politics? You could stack listening to politics podcasts onto your habit of brushing your teeth twice a day. But here's the thing – while habit stacking is an ingenious tool for building positive routines, it can inadvertently push us towards that slippery slope of multitasking and trying to cram more into every waking moment.

I noticed that when I went for a walk, I'd wear headphones to listen to my favourite podcasters, Kara Swisher and Scott Galloway. Why not hit my daily step goal and learn more about big tech at the same time? Or at the end of the day, getting into the bath, I'd have a book in one hand and my phone in the other, attempting to relax while also reading a philosophy book and catching up on social media. Sounds familiar? Think about it: when was the last time you truly enjoyed a single moment without feeling the urge to fill every spare second with additional distractions?

Don't get me wrong, I still love listening to podcasts when I'm walking around the park, or reading for ten minutes in the bath, but more often than not I now try to remove the layering of activities to become more aware of *what* I'm doing and *why* I'm doing it. If the aim of my morning walk is to exercise outside in nature and clear my mind, then I'll leave the headphones at home (sorry, Kara and Scott). When you commit to single-tasking, you open yourself up to a richer, more satisfying experience of life. It allows you to be fully immersed in conversations and interactions, which can enhance your relationships, improve your well-being and transform life's ordinary moments.

If you're working on a project, enjoying brunch with a friend or simply walking through the park, make the most of it by being present and aware. And the next time you're tempted to add a few more layers on top, remember that the myth of multitasking may seem appealing, but there is power in the simplicity of deciding to do one thing at a time.

2. Self-regulation

Essentially, self-regulation is the ability to manage our thoughts, emotions and behaviours in a way that aligns with our values and identity. Mastering self-regulation means learning how to act and react as you navigate the ups and downs of daily life. It's the ability to remain consistent regardless of what might be going on around you, instead of being at the mercy of random impulses, external circumstances and stressors.

When you're having one of those days where it feels like the universe has conspired against you – it's raining, the train is delayed, you've spilled coffee on your shirt, the dog walker just called to say he's sick – self-regulation is the tool that allows you to remain calm and reasonable instead of having a stress-induced meltdown (aka losing your shit). It's not about suppressing emotions or simply pretending everything is fine; rather, it's about cultivating a sense of resilience, composure and inner calm.

Coherent breathing is one of the practices that helps with self-regulation. This simple technique can provide immediate benefits for stress management and overall well-being. By practising it, you can effectively prevent stress from hijacking your state of mind.

Now, you might be wondering, *How much can breathing really do? I breathe all the time without even thinking about it.* And you're right, you do, but here's the thing: most of us aren't breathing effectively, especially if we're busy, rushing around and feeling stressed out. In this state, our breathing is dysfunctional. We usually take short shallow breaths, signalling to the brain that it's time to be alert, act quickly or even panic.

If you're sceptical about mindful breathing or breathwork as a practice then bear with me. This is not some woo-woo technique made up by TikTok yogis; this is a science-based practical tool you can use anywhere, anytime, to down-regulate your nervous system and bring yourself back to centre. Earlier on I referenced the body's *sympathetic* nervous system, also known as the 'fight or flight' response; this is our brain's go-to setting during times of high pressure and stress. Our body's physiological response in this state is an increase in heart rate, raised blood pressure and faster breathing.

In contrast, when we practise coherent breathing – in and out at a steady pace of around five to six breaths per minute – this activates the body's *parasympathetic* nervous system, often referred to as the 'rest and digest' mode. Within a few minutes of coherent breathing, the heart rate begins to lower and blood pressure returns to normal. Not only that, when we regularly practise this kind of self-regulation, we also cultivate coherence within ourselves. Studies have shown that coherent breathing can help with focus, emotional regulation and decision-making. When the parasympathetic nervous system is activated, we operate from a place that is more thoughtful and considered, rather than emotional and erratic. I often practise coherent breathing for a few minutes before I go into a meeting, after a heated disagreement, or any time I'm feeling overwhelmed or anxious.

On a recent flight from Rome to London, the seat belt sign lit up and the captain told us to expect mild turbulence. Initially, I wasn't worried – I'm a frequent flyer and turbulence is normal, especially when travelling in bad weather. But after twenty minutes of being rocked from side to side, I could feel my heart beating faster and I was becoming increasingly anxious and uncomfortable. So, knowing that there was literally nothing I could do to change the situation, I decided to take out my phone timer and began to practise coherent breathing, inhaling through the nose for five seconds and then exhaling through the nose for five seconds. Focusing on the timer made me less aware of each bump and bounce. As I continued to breathe slowly, my body immediately began to respond. You see, when our breathing pattern is 'low and slow', the body signals to the brain that we are safe, calm and resting. Coherent breathing is a powerful self-regulation tool that you can keep in your back pocket for whenever you need it.

The next time you start to feel overwhelmed by stress – whether it's a turbulent flight or a hectic day at work – remember to pause, reset and take a deep breath. The practice of self-regulation can help you to remain calm and composed when making decisions, as well as improving emotional resilience and overall well-being.

3. Sensory grounding

How many times have you heard the advice: 'Be present.' It's one of those things that sounds appealing, but it's much easier said than done, right? Our minds have this annoying tendency to either dwell on the past or anxiously project into the future, making it easy to feel disconnected from the present moment. Whether you're hustling in a demanding job or are an overwhelmed parent trying to juggle the chaos of family life, the advice to simply 'be present' in order to manage stress can seem – well, useless. If you're looking for a more practical solution, sensory grounding is a great place to start. So, what is it?

Sensory grounding is about tuning into your physical surroundings, using one of the five senses – sight, sound, touch, taste or smell – as a way to attach or ground yourself to the present moment. It's a way to cut through the noise of a racing mind and focus solely on the here and now. It can also be a helpful tool when negativity bias sends your mind spiralling into a loop of overwhelming thoughts and emotions. Grounding interrupts the pattern and allows you to reclaim control of your mental state. While it might sound like another hippie wellness concept, research shows that regular practice of sensory grounding techniques can reduce symptoms of anxiety and depression, enhancing overall mood.

Now, before you start picturing yourself wandering through a forest with bare feet, hold on. There are plenty of ways to practise sensory grounding that don't require you to remove your socks. You could start off with something as simple as smelling your morning coffee, a slice of freshly cut lemon or essential oils. For example, peppermint is a known energy booster; it can invigorate the mind and promote concentration and alertness. You could place a peppermint oil spray on your desk; when you sit down to start work, take a moment to spritz the room, then close your eyes and focus on the scent for 2–3 minutes. The idea is to observe and pay attention to the sensation of the smell. Notice the specific qualities. Is it cool or warm? Is it strong or subtle? You can further enhance the grounding experience by visualising the colour of peppermint leaves in your mind. If you start to get distracted, don't worry about it, just try to focus again on the smell for a minute or two.

Our sense of smell is closely linked to memory, which is why certain foods or fragrances can instantly remind us of a specific place or person. Just as certain scents can evoke memories of the past, we can also use scents intentionally to create new memories in the present. If you make smelling peppermint before you start to work a daily practice, not only are you deliberately using sensory grounding to feel less stressed in the moment, you're also creating a sensory memory. Over time you'll start to associate the smell of peppermint with a feeling of calm and focus. This ritual can help to alleviate the symptoms of stress before the day has even begun, preparing you for a day of calm decision-making.

Does sensory grounding really work? Well, like any mindful strategy, its effectiveness can vary from person to person and different techniques work better for different individuals, so it's worth experimenting to find what works best for you.

4. Social support

We all know that humans are social creatures by nature. We need social connection the way that plants need sunlight; it's essential for our mental and emotional well-being. When it comes to managing stress, having a solid support system in place can make all the difference. And let's not forget the practical benefits of being part of a group. Whatever the task, it's reassuring to know that you don't have to do it all alone. But social support isn't just about having help when life is challenging; it's also about having people who are there for the everyday struggles, changing seasons, wins and fails, and ups and downs of life too.

So how exactly can you harness the power of social support in your own life? Well, for starters, you have to be intentional about maintaining relationships. That means reaching out to friends and family on a regular basis, even when life gets busy. It could be sending a video message to a friend letting them know that you're thinking of them, or scheduling a monthly dinner date with your siblings to see them in person. It means putting in the effort, making time for those that matter, and showing up for people when they need you. Simple as that.

Last year I read a book titled *Sisterhood Heals*, written by clinical psychologist Dr Joy Harden Bradford. Her book dives deep into the importance of friendship, and finding connections with others who can share our experiences, struggles and celebrations. This is essential for everyone, irrespective of age, gender, class or ethnicity. We all need to feel connected and supported by others.

Support isn't just about offering a sympathetic ear; it's also about offering practical guidance when it's needed. Whether they're offering career advice, helping out with household tasks or simply acting as a sounding board for new ideas and high-stakes decisions, it's important to have people in your life who will support you. Those bonds are essential for navigating life's rollercoaster. But here's the thing, and the part we find the hardest: Offering help? Easy. Asking for it? Not so much.

The problem is, when you're not used to asking for help, you get very good at doing things on your own. As you become more capable and hyper-independent, this leads others to assume you don't need help from them and further reinforces your self-reliance. You've created this cycle yourself, but then you're left feeling frustrated and resentful when nobody offers to help you. The solution? Break the cycle, first by asking for help, and second by letting people know *how* they can help you.

For instance, suppose you find yourself in a position where you've just launched a new crowdfunding venture and you need help to raise awareness and money. You could reach out to three people in your professional network, letting them know about the project and asking each of them to share it with three more friends. When asking for support, be specific about what you need. People are more likely to help when they know exactly how they can contribute. Whether you're collecting feedback on a project, or seeking advice to make a decision, be clear about what you're asking for.

We need to normalise asking for help. And you know what? People are often more willing to lend a hand than you think. So, let's flip the script and stop adding additional unnecessary stress to our lives by attempting to go it alone. Remember that social connection is a two-way street. Reach out when you need support, and offer yours when others need it. A well-lived life is meant to be shared – even the stressful parts.

5. Seek solitude

In today's hyper-connected world, solitude is becoming increasingly rare. Regardless of whether you consider yourself to be an introvert or an extrovert, whether you're from a big family or grew up as an only child, solitude can be a way to retreat from overstimulation as well as being a reliable antidote to overwhelm and stress.

Solitude isn't just about being physically alone; it's about intentionally creating moments to mentally detach from devices and the distractions of notifications, emails and social media updates, allowing your mind to rest and recharge. Not only that, solitude also provides an opportunity for deep introspection and self-reflection. In quiet moments spent alone, we have space to think, consider how we feel, and gain clarity about ourselves and our lives.

My lifestyle means I spend a lot of time with other people; I have kids, an active social life, and my work requires me to interact with a lot of people. I travel frequently, and I generally enjoy the company of others. However, I recognise the need to incorporate solitude into my routine as a way for my mind and body to truly rest. Creating moments for solitude in your schedule requires intentional effort and discipline, but the benefits far outweigh the costs.

A practical strategy to incorporate solitude into your routine is to schedule regular solo activities that are restorative and nourishing. These might include going to an art gallery, having lunch in a café, walking, doodling or watching a movie. Whatever you choose to do as a solo activity, try to fully immerse yourself in the task and go 'tech free' for a while to avoid any interruptions. You might find it useful to pencil the date and time into your diary as a way to ensure it remains a priority.

After spending a few hours alone in my kitchen, batch-cooking and singing along to Motown hits, my energy is renewed and I'm noticeably less stressed. I regularly go for long walks by myself, and sometimes I go to my favourite Italian restaurant and enjoy an indulgent dinner for one. The next time you feel overwhelmed by the demands of modern life, carve out time to be alone, and give yourself the space to recharge and replenish your energy.

The decision-making matrix

At the start of this chapter, I mentioned how reading is good but doing is better. So here it is. You've read this far, and if you're still with me then I'm sure you're ready to start doing. So let's roll up our sleeves and start putting the pieces of this puzzle together.

I've created a decision-making matrix that you can use to weigh up your choices based on your values, your sense of joy, your vision of success, and the impact you want to make. It's a framework that allows you to assess and evaluate each important decision based on your own personal criteria. Think of it as a weighted scoring model or a decision calculator, except instead of numbers, you're plugging in your ideas, values, goals and what truly matters to you.

I've tried and tested this method in a variety of situations. I've used it to help business clients, start-up founders, friends and family members – as well as using it to make some of the most important decisions in my own life. Trust me, when used correctly, it can provide you with a clear and reliable answer to virtually any decision. Here's how it works:

	Values	Joy	Success	Impact	Total
1					
2					

THE DECISION-MAKING MATRIX

Step 1
Identify the decision that needs to be made and the different options available. Write these down and keep it as simple and clear as possible.

Step 2
Using your predefined criteria – Values, Joy, Success, Impact – evaluate each option and give it a score from 1 to 5. For instance, scoring a 1 for Values would mean this option aligns poorly with your core values. Scoring a 5 for Impact would mean this option has the potential to create a significant positive impact. Scoring a 1 for Joy would mean this option is likely to bring minimal joy to your life. And so on.

Next, write down one or two sentences to explain your rationale.

When we use a numerical scale, it helps us to see things more clearly and objectively. Giving each option a score lets us directly compare and contrast them side by side so we can make an informed decision. Lastly, providing a reason highlights your thought process and gives you further clarity, ultimately leading to a confident final decision.

MAKING DECISIONS IN THE REAL WORLD

Step 3
Calculate and compare your total scores. The decision will be made by whichever one scores the most.

Let's look at an example . . .

Step 1 – Identify and define
Let's say you're trying to decide if you should stay in your current job role as a copywriter for a digital magazine or leave and work as a freelance copywriter? You've talked about it in the past with friends but never really given it enough thought or consideration. Now, you're ready to make a decision using the structured approach outlined above.

Step 2 – Evaluate

- ***Values:*** *How much does my current role align with my personal values?*

CURRENT JOB
SCORE: 3
REASON: While my current job aligns with some of my values such as teamwork and creativity, I'm often required to write short articles with clickbait

titles to increase views and virality online. This means I have to compromise the quality of my writing as I have so many deadlines and not enough time to meet them. This feels as though I'm compromising my own values of integrity and authenticity.

FREELANCE

SCORE: 4

REASON: Freelance work would allow me to write my own articles and weekly newsletter. Plus, I'll seek out clients and projects that are aligned with my personal interests.

- *Joy: How much do I enjoy my current job?*

CURRENT JOB

SCORE: 3

REASON: I love the people I work with but the work itself has become repetitive and uninspiring.

FREELANCE

SCORE: 3

REASON: I'll enjoy having more varied work but I won't enjoy the inconsistency of freelancing.

- *Success: How much does my current role reflect my definition of success?*

MAKING DECISIONS IN THE REAL WORLD

CURRENT JOB
SCORE: 2
REASON: My current definition of success is to have more agency and control of my time and my schedule. Even though I earn a reliable consistent income, I currently have no work-life balance.

FREELANCE
SCORE: 4
REASON: I'll be able to create my own schedule and work remotely. I have already saved some money, so I can afford to earn less for a while. Freelance work feels like a step closer to creating the work-life balance that I want.

- ***Impact:*** *How much impact can I have in my current job?*

CURRENT JOB
SCORE: 3
REASON: The main agenda is set by my boss. I have some input, but overall my impact is limited.

FREELANCE
SCORE: 5
REASON: Writing articles and newsletters without limitations means I can discuss topics and issues that are important to me. I know I can have an impact on my community. (This is very important to me.)

> Now it's time to tally up the total scores. Staying in your current job scored a total of 11 out of 20, whereas leaving to work as a freelancer scored a total of 16 out of 20.

Using this framework and example, based on the final scores it's clear that it is possible to leave the job and pursue freelance work with confidence. Of course, decision-making isn't always straightforward. It doesn't mean you will be 100 per cent certain that it's the right thing to do, or that now is exactly the right time. There will always be unknowns and a degree of uncertainty; that's life. However, using this structured approach helps to weigh up the pros and cons objectively. The final decision takes into consideration what really matters, and is aligned with your personal values and goals.

It's also worth remembering Decision-Making 101: this is not a closed-door decision that, once made, is impossible to undo. In this hypothetical scenario, if you spent a year pursuing freelance work and found yourself rethinking your decision, you could reverse it and go back to employment.

The answer here is clear: with a score of 16, it's a YES.

WHAT IF THERE ARE MORE THAN TWO OPTIONS?

If you have more than two options to consider, simply repeat Steps 2 and 3 for each option, comparing total scores at the end. Take your time and ensure each option is evaluated objectively against your criteria. The same rules apply: the highest score is the most favourable option.

WHAT IF THERE'S A TIEBREAKER?

In the unlikely event of a tie, revisit Chapter 1 and consider the sixth rule of engagement: trust your gut. Even after weighing up the pros and cons of multiple outcomes, some decisions still require that you listen to your intuition and make the decision that *feels* right based on all the information available. Remember, no decision-making method is foolproof, but using a structured and thoughtful approach means you are far more likely to be satisfied with the final outcome.

THE GOLDEN RULE

Here is one final golden rule that I apply when using this decision-making matrix. It's simple yet powerful. If anything scores a 0 in any category, it makes the decision an immediate no. A score of 0 means that you can't think of a single good reason to pursue it. Nothing at all. Therefore, it's automatically disqualified. Life's too short to waste time on things that offer nothing of value, joy, success or impact.

The decision-making matrix I've presented here isn't just a template to illustrate the point; it's a strategic tool that you can use to transform how you make decisions. Rather than surrendering to chance or luck, use this matrix to turn thoughtful consideration into decisive action and proactively shape your future. By adopting this approach, you can eliminate distractions and gain clarity on *why* and *how* you make decisions, ensuring each choice is aligned with your core values and goals. Use the matrix anytime you want to feel less overwhelmed by the decision you are making and more confident in your final choice.

Navigating effective decision-making in our fast-paced world demands more than just theoretical knowledge; it requires real-life practical application. Remember this: by integrating mindful practices into your daily routine and employing a strategic framework, you may not be able to eliminate stress and other distractions entirely, but you can find ways of remaining calm and so make rational decisions even in demanding situations.

Conclusion

Embracing uncertainty, mistakes and regrets

Embracing uncertainty

The only thing that is constant in life? Change. Life isn't static – it's the changes, the highs and lows, that add contrast, colour and depth to our lives. Change brings growth and development, new opportunities and challenges. Those unexpected moments that just happen by accident and catch us off guard? For better or for worse, they make life memorable. Uncertainty comes bundled with change, and it's sort of a package deal – you can't have one without the other – but the 'unknown' doesn't have to be feared and it doesn't have to hold you back.

In the context of decision-making, uncertainty is the unsettling notion that we lack complete knowledge about all potential future outcomes. We want to know what's behind each door before we choose which one to open. Predictability is the antidote to uncertainty. We look for certainty because it gives us a sense of assurance and security. That's why many of us create routines that are repeatable; they provide us with structure. But life, with its unpredictability, chaos and mess, more often than not refuses to adhere to our neatly laid-out plans. Imagine meticulously planning a wedding down to the smallest detail – from the grand venue to the beautiful flowers, you've left no stone unturned. The guest list is carefully curated and the menu is tailored to perfection. You've created a detailed schedule to ensure everything will unfold seamlessly. Yet, on the morning of the wedding, you wake up to dark clouds and torrential rain. Despite all of your preparation, there's nothing you can do to change it; it's pure bad luck.

The weather – along with interest rates and genetics – is in a box labelled 'uncontrollables'. When you accept that some things in life just are the way they are, you'll stop wasting time and energy trying to change them. You know you can't change your height, shoe size or England's chances of winning the World Cup final, right? There are so many moments in life that highlight our limitations and our inability to control every outcome. So why stress over them when you could redirect that energy towards things that you *can* change?

Learning to embrace uncertainty is a skill worth mastering, because there will always be variables beyond your control. No matter how much information you have or how well you plan, life's unpredictability will throw you into situations where your plans fall short. Without a tolerance for ambiguity, uncertainty can be a stumbling block that derails your confidence and leaves you feeling stuck. If you want to become more comfortable making decisions in uncertain situations, consider scenario and contingency planning.

Scenario and contingency planning

Scenario and contingency planning are practical strategies for dealing with uncertainty. Both are common practice when making decisions in business, and we can easily apply these principles to our personal lives too. Rather than relying on a single prediction – *if I choose x, then y will happen* – these hypothetical planning strategies encourage you to explore multiple possible futures and devise a plan to handle each one. By preparing for various scenarios, you're not just hoping for the best, you're being proactive and anticipating life's curve balls instead of feeling blindsided when things change.

Scenario planning involves envisioning a variety of different outcomes that could unfold. For example, when making the decision whether to launch a new product, a business founder could consider some what-if scenarios. *What if our supply chain is delayed? What if a competitor releases the exact same product? What if we sell out on day one of release? How quickly can we produce and ship more?* And so on. By exploring these different possibilities, not only can you spot potential opportunities, risks and make more informed decisions, you also become more adaptable. This kind of thoughtful preparation provides you and those around you with additional confidence, as it's clear that decisions have been made with consideration and rationale.

This strategy can also be applied in our personal lives, simply by asking: *What if x, y or z were to happen?* Imagining future scenarios gives you a head start if and when things don't unfold as you expect them to. By visualising your future self in each hypothetical scenario, you'll feel better prepared in real life too.

Contingency planning, on the other hand, is all about preparing for the worst-case scenarios. It's essentially having a back-up plan in case things go south. Whether an unexpected bill or a sudden drop in demand, contingency planning helps you to identify potential setbacks and develop strategies to mitigate their impact. It's sort of like having an insurance policy for life.

Think about it – what do you typically do when plans suddenly change? Say your flight has been cancelled, or your child is sick and can't go to school, or the buyer pulls out of your house sale. Panic? Pray for a miracle? Or do you start to look for an alternative solution? Do you have a back-up plan? Do you find another way? Contingency planning can act as your safety net when things go wrong, and provide peace of mind in times of uncertainty.

In the end, even the best decision-makers must be willing to adjust their plans as circumstances evolve. It's virtually impossible to make a decision with complete certainty of what will happen as a consequence. To put this into practice, take a moment to think about a recent decision you made, and consider how scenario and contingency planning could have enhanced the decision-making process. What alternative scenarios could you have explored? What contingency plans could you have put in place? This exercise, if practised regularly, will help you to develop a more proactive approach to decision-making. Embracing uncertainty and planning for the unexpected are essential skills that will enable you to make informed, confident decisions – and to adapt quickly when things inevitably change. Most people want to wait until they are certain before they act. But you will never be certain of anything *until* you act.

Plan for the worst, hope for the best, and try to approach the unknown with a sense of curiosity and optimism. Some of the best things in life happen when we least expect them.

Mistakes and regrets

While uncertainty casts a shadow over decisions we're yet to make in the future, regrets come from choices we've made in our past. Let's face it, no matter how diligently we strive to make mindful decisions, mistakes are inevitable. Occasionally we'll act impulsively and sometimes make a choice that we later regret. But that's just part of being human. I'm pretty sure we all have regrets – maybe not the kind that keep us up at night, but those uncomfortable feelings about a past choice that make us wish we could turn back the clock on a 'bad decision'.

There are some people who boldly claim to have 'no regrets', and some even go as far as tattooing those two words on their skin. (I can't help but wonder how many of them ironically later regret that choice!) But let's be real, declaring that you have 'no regrets' is like saying with absolute certainty: 'I've lived a mistake-free life.' Perhaps our reluctance to admit our regrets comes from a fear of shining a light on our imperfections and past failures. In a world that continually glorifies perfection, it's understandable that we feel the need to sweep our mistakes under the rug. But what if we reevaluate our stance on regrets, and start using them to highlight what we care about, and where we took a wrong turn or missed a good opportunity. What if we could accept that regrets are an essential part of life? Even if we don't like the idea of embracing them, let's at least be willing to tolerate them. We can do this by acknowledging that, ultimately, the choices we regret can help us to make better decisions in the future. It's okay to admit when you've made a mistake; let failure move you forwards.

Attempting to avoid regret is a trap that keeps us stuck. When making decisions, sometimes we hesitate, and even when we are presented with a sufficient and 'good enough' option, we are reluctant to accept it. Instead, we continue our search in the hope that we'll discover something better down the road. We ask ourselves: *What if I took this job/dated this person/bought this car today, only for an even better option to appear tomorrow?* This phenomenon even has a name – FOBO, the fear of better options.

It's okay to admit when you've made a mistake; let failure move you forwards.

You're probably familiar with the term FOMO – the fear of missing out. You might think it's a relatively recent phenomenon that has been amplified by Instagram, but the truth is, FOMO is a normal part of the human experience – and it has always been. Whether you're attempting to keep up with the Joneses – or the modern-day equivalent, keep up with the Kardashians – the root sentiment remains the same. The fear of missing out comes from comparing our lives to others' and feeling inadequate in the process. FOMO makes you feel bad because no matter what you have, seeing someone else with more leaves you feeling dissatisfied. Give a four-year-old a scoop of ice cream and they'll be happy – that is until they see another kid with two scoops of ice cream topped with chocolate sprinkles. This is simply a fixture of the human psyche.

Think of FOMO and FOBO as brothers. FOMO is the loud, attention-grabbing elder sibling, while FOBO is subtle and lesser-known – yet equally dangerous when you're trying to make a decision. You see, FOBO plants a seed of doubt and hesitation in your mind, and if you're convinced there might be a better option waiting around the corner, you'll hold back for as long as possible and put off reaching a conclusion and making a choice. Your unwillingness to settle for anything due to FOBO is a curse that prevents you from choosing anything at all.

One surefire way to sabotage your peace of mind is to make up an elaborate story about what could have been. *If only I'd taken that job, moved to that town, bought that flat or ordered the soup instead, then my entire life could have been different!* We

CONCLUSION

torture ourselves with visions of an alternative reality where everything falls perfectly into place. The unlucky one finds the golden ticket, the underdogs win the championship, the geeky girl removes her glasses and gets the guy. (Clearly, I grew up watching too many 1990s movies.)

Instead of dwelling on past decisions and daydreaming about what might have been, why not shift your focus? Rather than asking *Did I make the right decision?* ask yourself *How can I make this decision right?* Remember that it's possible to accept the choices you have made, forge ahead and make the best of them. Ultimately, the pursuit of a perfect life or a regret-free existence is a futile one. The person who never made a mistake, never made anything.

Making decisions that matter

Every decision requires us to sacrifice one option for another. On Friday evening I can either watch a movie with my kids or I can stay in my office and continue working; I cannot do both – remember that multitasking is a myth. Choosing one doesn't mean that I don't care about the other, but it's a choice that must be made. The act of choosing will affirm my values, priorities and eventually my life.

Since the word 'decide' literally means 'to cut off', in order to make a choice we must cut off and eliminate the other options. When you choose one thing, you have to accept that you are giving up the alternative, leaving certain possibilities behind – and this is not a bad thing. In fact, embracing this can liberate you from overwhelming indecision. This is what allows you to make a choice and then commit to it. To declare: 'This is what I care about. This is where I'll invest my time, energy, focus and love. *This* is what matters to me.'

If you piece together the countless decisions you make throughout your life, you'll see that each one has contributed to its trajectory in one way or another. In the end, it's not about how many decisions turned out to be right or wrong, but rather how you feel about those decisions that counts. Perhaps the true measure of a decision is not the final outcome, but rather its intention and the narratives you choose to believe about the end result. When you know that you have made decisions rooted in your values and the things that bring you joy, and when you align your actions to the pursuit of success and the impact you want to have on others, then you can stand tall knowing that you've stayed true to yourself. While the outcome of any decision remains uncertain, the power of choice is a gift you get to use every day.

Throughout the year that I dedicated to writing this book, I spoke to countless people about decision-making. I asked mentors, friends, family members and colleagues to tell me about the decisions that had shaped their lives, the chances they took and the choices they were proud of, as well as any lasting regrets.

I even found myself speaking to a man sitting beside me on a flight from London to Los Angeles. When I told him about this book, it sparked a fascinating conversation.

He spoke about his life, career and family. We talked about everything from luck and serendipity to timing, talent and personal ambition. Thank you, Andy in seat 12C, for sharing your ideas and experiences with me.

The conversations I had ranged from late-night phone calls to walks around the park, and long personal emails to chance encounters at 30,000 feet. When given the chance, most people have wonderful stories to tell about the decisions that have shaped their lives. But these are not just stories; they are lessons we can all learn from.

It's evident to me now that there is no guaranteed formula for success – no blueprint for living a life without mistakes or regret. There's no singular moment, right or wrong choice, make-or-break decision that defines who we are.

And so, I thought the best way to conclude this book would be to share some of these stories with you. I'm incredibly grateful to those who took the time to open their minds and hearts to me, sharing their stories with candour and vulnerability. Some of the contributors would like to remain anonymous, so small details may have been changed.

Q: Tell me about a decision that shaped your life?

Ten years ago, I made a pivotal decision that forever changed my life. I decided to work with friends and establish my own youth charity. Driven by a desire for autonomy and a passion for making a difference in my community, I embarked on this journey with enthusiasm and optimism. This decision allowed me to work directly within my own community, addressing the needs of young people and fostering a sense of belonging and purpose.

Setting up the charity provided me with invaluable opportunities to learn and grow. I developed new skills in running a business, managing teams, and measuring the impact of our initiatives. These experiences have been incredibly rewarding. The ability to shape our programmes and see the direct impact of our work on the lives of young people has been immensely fulfilling.

However, my journey has not been without its challenges. When I made the decision to start the charity, I was unaware of the many difficulties I would face. Running a charity in a capitalist society is fraught with precarity, particularly around securing funding. I also encountered community trauma that was deeply affecting. I have found that there are many areas of running a charity that I don't enjoy, but are essential to keep it going. These challenges tested my resilience and required me to adapt and learn continually.

Reflecting on this journey, I am grateful for the decision I made. It has provided me with a unique sense of purpose and the opportunity to make a tangible difference. Yet, I also recognize that I did not fully anticipate the consequences of this decision. The difficulties have been significant, but they have also been part of the growth and learning process. Ultimately, this decision has shaped me into a more resilient and committed individual, dedicated to making a positive impact in my community.

—**Male, 38**

A decision I regret is not going to Iran to see my mum after she had surgery to remove a tumour from her brain. She insisted that I not go until she felt better. The next time I saw her, she was in a coma, having had a fall in the night, and sadly she passed away. Since then, I have followed my instinct and never missed an opportunity to be with my loved ones. You never know what is around the corner.

—**Female, 48**

A pivotal decision that changed my life was calling off my engagement. It wasn't an easy thing to do, especially as I felt a lot of pressure from my family's expectations. As the wedding date approached, I felt overwhelmed at the thought of committing my life to a person I didn't truly love, but it felt too late to go back. The fear of disappointing everyone around me made me feel trapped.

When I finally made the decision, I was sitting in an airport, waiting for a flight and surrounded by strangers. As I watched the interactions of travellers, I thought about what I wanted my future to look like. In the end, I chose my own happiness and called off the engagement.

The aftermath was difficult, and even though my friends and parents were shocked and disappointed, I knew it was the right decision because I felt free.

—**Male, 35**

As someone who works in the well-being industry, it's easy to think the positive behaviours such as movement, nutrition, sleep and recovery would be enough to be 'well'. However, it is clear from my understanding of well-being that leading a life of purpose is of equal or greater value. During lockdown, there was a moment where I was delivering work to a premium client in the luxury sector and facing obstacles in providing the service standard they expected. Luxury work is challenging at the best of times but even more so with Covid restrictions in place. At the same time, in a shared office, my partner was working in legal aid where she was trying to convince a challenged individual not to take their own life. I am pleased to say that she succeeded in the intervention. The comparison between the impact of our work was stark and left me cold for several days.

I began to understand how important it was for my work to contribute in a more meaningful way. I made a decision to leave a wonderful, collaborative place of work, with stability and financial security, to venture out into the uncertainty of self-employment. This decision was not taken easily during a Covid crisis while supporting a household with two small children. The catalyst was wanting to pursue work that would fulfil a broader well-being objective, while closely aligning with my personal values. I only have one existence, and when it comes to the end, I will ask myself a vital question: *What did I contribute?* I still sit in the shadow of my partner's work, but I feel a greater purpose in my work. This

CONCLUSION

has brought enormous personal satisfaction and a breadth of work beyond my initial imagination.

—**Male, 46**

When I think of a decision that has shaped my life, I think of the decision to love my partner. Many people think love happens to them or is decided for them, hence the term 'falling', but I think you decide and that we are very much active participants in the decision to love. After many years of making bad choices, I met a man who was really kind, thoughtful, fun and was really into me. We were aligned on so many things and I remember trying to figure out my feelings: did I love him? One day, I decided I did. It doesn't sound very romantic when you put it like this, but I chose to love him and that moment has shaped everything since.

I have a true life companion and we are designing the life we want together. I am no longer making choices on my own, and that means his influence and needs are now reflected in what I want. He champions me and makes me feel that anything is possible, so I'm bolder in the direction I'm taking my life. And finally, I am no longer alone. I start and end every day with him by my side and that never gets boring. I will never take that for granted.

—**Female, 45**

The best decision I ever made was to embrace the concept of minimalism. It started with a book called *Discovery of LESS* by Chris Lovett. As I read the book I felt an immediate shift in my mindset. I was sitting in my messy flat and I couldn't wait to start decluttering. Not long after, I watched a Netflix documentary called *The Minimalists: Less Is Now*, and this spurred me on further. Within a few months, I had sold half of my clothes, books, old laptops and phones. I even gave away an exercise bike that I had barely used. It felt great to no longer have so much stuff. My wardrobe is no longer over-packed and my kitchen is tidy. I can't recommend it enough.

After reading that book, I told a few friends about my decision to adopt minimalism. They laughed, assuming it wouldn't last. Three years on and I can honestly say that living with less has changed my life for the better. I feel less overwhelmed and less distracted. Last Christmas, I convinced my family to embrace the idea too. Instead of buying gifts, we spent a day cooking food and drinking wine together. I can confidently say that it's not just a passing phase, it's a way of life now. If you make one decision to change the way you live, don't be surprised when everything else changes too.

—**Anonymous**

Deciding to start therapy at the age of fifty-five was a decision that has transformed my life. After years of neglecting self-care and putting other people's needs first, I've finally started to believe that I matter too. This has led me to a healthier lifestyle because I now make time for regular exercise. This year, I'm going on my first-ever yoga retreat. I feel like I've just started to live my life.

—**Female, 55**

CONCLUSION

After years of trying to conceive I was told by my doctor that I would need to have uterine surgery and it would be very risky for me to have a baby. It was a scary decision but one that I'm glad I made because now I have my son. It was the best decision of my life!

—**Female, 42**

In 1973 I was living in Japan while working as a foreign diplomat for the Iraq embassy. I attended an exhibition where I met a beautiful Peruvian woman. I looked at her and I thought, this is it! I came to her and I said hello and we spoke for a moment. I asked her, 'What time do you finish work? I would like to take you out for dinner.' She hesitated for a moment before agreeing to meet with me. After that day, we spent a week together and it was wonderful. She even introduced me to her father, but we knew that after this week, she had to leave Japan and return to Peru. She said, 'You have to come with me.' I considered many things in my mind but I knew quickly it was not the right decision at that time in my life to go with her.

When I reflect on that decision, I have no regrets. I don't know what that life would have been – it could have been fantastic but I wouldn't have lived the life that I have lived and seen all I have seen. They say, 'We will never know about the doors that we didn't open or the path we didn't walk,' and this is absolutely true. That is why I am satisfied and do not regret my decision.

—**Male, 83**

ACKNOWLEDGEMENTS

First and foremost, I want to acknowledge the writers, thinkers and authors who contribute so generously. In moments of doubt, it's because of your courage to share your ideas so boldly and honestly that I'm able to share mine. Sharmadean Reid, Emma Gannon, Oliver Burkeman, Scott Galloway, Sarah Knight and so many more – your work continues to inspire me. Unknowingly, you have been my mentors. You've taught me to believe in the power of my own ideas.

To my husband, Sam. Thank you for bringing me cups of coffee and runny eggs in the mornings, and for taking the children swimming on Saturdays so I could spend a few hours alone in the office. I'm sure you're glad that it's finally done! Thank you for your endless patience, love and support. Jude, Alice and Ferdi, I hope you'll enjoy reading this book one day.

To the incredible women in my life – Aicha, Hayley, Natasha, Tara, Rachael, Mitra – each of you reflects what's possible when women support women. You show up, you inspire me and you bring out the best in me. I love you all!

Then there's the team behind-the-scenes, the people who helped me take this book from an idea to something real.

ACKNOWLEDGEMENTS

Sophie, Flora, Lydia, Ryn, Laurie, Anna, and a special thank you to Danai. I know working with a detail-oriented Virgo isn't always easy! But I'm grateful that you stuck with me and together we've made something I'm really proud of. Thank you for your hard work, dedication and belief in me throughout this project. This book is better because of each one of you.

Finally, I need to thank the people who make all of this worthwhile – the readers, the podcast listeners and the incredible online community that supports my work. Every time you leave a comment, send a message or share your thoughts, I'm reminded of why I do this. Behind all the screens, there are real people and it's YOU I think about every time I sit down to write. You are the reason I do this work, even when it's hard, and I'm so grateful for your constant support. Thank you for being a part of this journey with me. I hope this book inspires you to believe in the power of your ideas, to take action and to make Decisions That Matter.

In the end, this book is a collection of decisions – choices made, chances and opportunities taken. And none of it would have been possible without the people I've mentioned here. So thank you, all of you.

NOTES

INTRODUCTION

p. 3 'we even walk faster . . .', Fiona MacRae, 'Pace of life speeds up as study reveals we're walking faster than ever', *Daily Mail*, 2 May 2007, https://dailymail.co.uk/sciencetech/article-452046/Pace-life-speeds-study-reveals-walking-faster-ever.html

p. 4 'It's estimated that the average person . . .', Amanda Reill, 'A simple way to make better decisions', *Harvard Business Review*, 5 December 2023, https://hbr.org/2023/12/a-simple-way-to-make-better-decisions

p. 5 'viewers spend an average of . . .', George Winslow, 'Study: Streamers now wasting record amounts of time finding something to watch', *TV Tech*, 28 August 2023, https://www.tvtechnology.com/news/study-streamers-now-wasting-record-amounts-of-time-finding-something-to-watch

CHAPTER 1: RULES OF ENGAGEMENT

p. 28 'A study published in the journal *Cognition* . . .', María Juliana Leone et al., 'Time to decide: Diurnal variations

NOTES

on the speed and quality of human decisions', *Cognition*, January 2017, https://www.sciencedirect.com/science/article/abs/pii/S0010027716302414

p. 29 '"Decision fatigue" is a well-documented phenomenon . . .', Dan Pilat and Dr Sekoul Krastev, 'Why do we make worse decisions at the end of the day?', The Decision Lab, https://thedecisionlab.com/biases/decision-fatigue

p. 29 'judges were more likely to . . .', The Decision Lab, https://thedecisionlab.com/biases/decision-fatigue

p. 29 'For example, a study . . .' Weinshall-Margel & Shapard, 'Overlooked factors in the analysis of parole decisions', *PNAS*, October 2011, https://www.pnas.org/doi/full/10.1073/pnas.1110910108#body-ref-r1

p. 32 'During his presidency, Barack Obama . . .', Drake Baer, 'Always wear the same suit: Obama's presidential productivity secrets', *Fast Company*, 12 February 2014, https://www.fastcompany.com/3026265/always-wear-the-same-suit-obamas-presidential-productivity-secrets

p. 32 'Matilda Kahl, an art director . . .', Matilda Kahl, 'Why I wear the exact same thing to work every day', *Harper's Bazaar*, 3 April 2015, https://harpersbazaar.com/culture/features/a10441/why-i-wear-the-same-thing-to-work-everday/

p. 39 '"Nobody really wants to hear criticism . . ."', Kim Scott, *Radical Candor*

p. 46 Intuition research, Nathaniel Barr, 'Intuition, reason and creativity: An integrative dual-process

NOTES

perspective', April 2017, https://researchgate.net/publication/315803868_Intuition_reason_and_creativity_An_integrative_dual-process_perspective

CHAPTER 2: VALUES

p. 80   'Research shows that it only takes three seconds...', 'The three second social media rule', Marketing Essentials Lab, 2 December 2021, https://marketingessentialslab.com/%E2%80%A8the-three-second-social-media-rule/

p. 83   'analysed data on nearly 227,000 people...' Julie Corliss, 'Higher step counts linked to lower risk of heart-related death', *Harvard Health Publishing*, 1 November 2023, https://www.health.harvard.edu/heart-health/higher-step-counts-linked-to-lower-risk-of-heart-related-death

p. 87   Google, Disney and Tesla mission statements, The Business Model Analyst, https://businessmodelanalyst.com/google-mission-and-vision-statement/, The Walt Disney Company, https://thewaltdisneycompany.com/about/, Aluminium Stewardship Initiative, https://aluminium-stewardship.org/about-asi/members/Tesla-Inc-

CHAPTER 3: JOY

p. 96   '"happiness leads to healthier behaviours..."', American Heart Association, https://www.heart.org/en/

NOTES

university-hospitals-harrington-heart-and-vascular/
how-happiness-affects-health

p. 96   'In fact, research into . . .', Andrew Steptoe, 'Happiness and health', *Annual Review of Public Health*, 40, 2019, pp. 339–359, https://doi.org/10.1146/annurev-publhealth-040218-044150

p. 96   'People who have lived in . . .' Public Health England, 'Health matters: reducing health inequalities in mental illness, 18 December 2018, https://www.gov.uk/government/publications/health-matters-reducing-health-inequalities-in-mental-illness/health-matters-reducing-health-inequalities-in-mental-illness

p. 97   'In 2017, a meta-analysis looked at . . .', N. Martín-María et al., 'The impact of subjective well-being on mortality: A meta-analysis of longitudinal studies in the general population', *Psychosomatic Medicine*, 79(5), 2017, pp. 565–75, https://journals.lww.com/psychosomaticmedicine/abstract/2017/06000/the_impact_of_subjective_well_being_on_mortality_.10.aspx

p. 98   'The 2023–24 edition found that . . .', PureGym, *The UK Fitness Report – 2023/24 Gym Statistics*, https://www.puregym.com/blog/uk-fitness-report-gym-statistics/

p. 100   '"there's a big mistake . . ."', Arthur C. Brooks, in conversation with Tim Ferriss on the *Tim Ferriss Show* podcast, 11 September 2023

p. 100   'the Positive and Negative Affect Schedule . . .', arthurbrooks.com, https://arthurbrooks.com/hubfs/PANAS%20Lesson%20Plan-1.pdf

NOTES

p. 107   'This bias was discovered . . .' Michael Shermer, '2017: What scientific term or concept ought to be more widely known?', *Edge*, https://www.edge.org/response-detail/27025

p. 107   'Research conducted at Penn State . . .', Penn State, 'Linguistics may be clue to emotions, according to Penn State research', 20 January 2005, https://www.psu.edu/news/research/story/linguistics-may-be-clue-emotions-according-penn-state-research/

p. 107   'This form of selective attention . . .' *The Decision Lab*, 'Why is the news always so depressing?', https://thedecisionlab.com/biases/negativity-bias

CHAPTER 4: SUCCESS

p. 127   'Bezos talks about the concept . . .', Ram Charan, 'How Amazon does it: Decision making inside the world's most daring digital company', *Chief Executive*, https://chiefexecutive.net/how-amazon-does-it-decision-making-inside-the-worlds-most-daring-digital-company/

p. 155   'When I spoke to . . .' Thomas Curran, in conversation with me on the *Power Hour* podcast, 30 May 2023

CHAPTER 5: IMPACT

p. 172   'Godin mentioned how saying . . .', Seth Godin, in conversation with Simon Sinek on *A Bit of Optimism*, 14 March 2023

NOTES

p. 177   '"You're the average . . ."', Aimee Groth, 'You're the average of the five people you spend the most time with', *Business Insider*, 24 July 2012, https://www.businessinsider.com/jim-rohn-youre-the-average-of-the-five-people-you-spend-the-most-time-with-2012-7

p. 180   '"Asking questions is key. . ."', Charles Duhigg, in conversation with me on the *Power Hour* podcast, 27 February 2024

p. 188   'Research supports this notion . . .', Paris Stevens, 'The 2021 post-lockdown friends & happiness in the workplace survey', *Wildgoose*, 9 June 2021, https://wearewildgoose.com/uk/news/friends-happiness-in-the-workplace-survey/

p. 195   '"We're living in a time of artificial intimacy"', Esther Perel, in conversation with Scott Galloway on *The Prof G Pod*, 8 April 2021

CHAPTER 6: MAKING DECISIONS IN THE REAL WORLD

p. 210   'A recent study linked excessive screen time . . .', Gadi Lissak, 'Adverse physiological and psychological effects of screen time on children and adolescents: Literature review and case study', *Environmental Research*, July 2018, https://pubmed.ncbi.nlm.nih.gov/29499467/

p. 212   'Holmes and Rahe stress scale . . .', Wikipedia entry, https://en.wikipedia.org/wiki/Holmes_and_Rahe_stress_scale

NOTES

p. 215   '"habit stacking" . . .', James Clear, *Atomic Habits*, Random House Business, 2018

p. 217   'Coherent breathing is one . . .' Zaccaro et al., 'How breath-control can change your life: A systematic review on psycho-physiological correlates of slow breathing', *Frontiers in Human Neuroscience*, September 2018, https://www.ncbi.nlm.nih.gov/pmc/articles/PMC6137615/

p. 220   'research shows that regular practice . . .', Julie Marks, 'Grounding exercises: Using 5 senses for anxiety relief', Psych Central, 8 October 2021, https://psychcentral.com/anxiety/using-the-five-senses-for-anxiety-relief

p. 222   'Last year I read . . .', Dr Joy Harden Bradford, *Sisterhood Heals*, #Merky Books, 2023

Adrienne Adhami is a leading well-being coach and keynote speaker best known for the motivational podcast *Power Hour* and for co-hosting the *Modern Wellness* podcast.

In addition, she is a sought-after brand advisor, specialising in well-being technology, strategy and innovation. She has delivered workshops and keynotes for some of the world's leading brands, including Apple, Spotify, Bupa and Range Rover. Her expertise spans a wide range of topics, from enhancing productivity and achieving high performance to goal-setting and decision-making.

Her debut book, *Power Hour*, was published in 2020 and has since been translated into four languages around the world. Listed as one of the 'Top 25 Black Entrepreneurs to Watch' in 2023 by HSBC and UKBBS, Adrienne is a trailblazer who continues to inspire individuals and organisations to reach their full potential. *Decisions That Matter* is her second book.